The State of Feminist Social Work

D0145003

Much has been written about relating feminism to social work. In particular, proponents of feminist social work have focused on the role of women social workers in developing distinctive forms of practice, rooted in a commitment to egalitarian relationships with women service users. *The State of Feminist Social Work* challenges the limitations of this perspective at a time of major change in social work's policies, organisation and day-to-day practice.

Tracing key ideas in feminist social work from the 1970s through to the present day, and using data from interviews with women social workers, this book draws out tensions between the literature and the experiences of women social workers. In doing so, it:

- highlights the significance of social work's location in the state
- enables the experiences of women social workers to be explored and placed within their organisational context
- reveals diverse identities, identifications and stances amongst women social workers
- critically examines the current state of feminist social work

The State of Feminist Social Work provides an important appraisal of the subject and is essential reading for all those with an interest in feminism and social work theory, practice and education.

Vicky White teaches and researches in the School of Health and Social Studies at the University of Warwick. In addition to substantial experience in social work education at qualification, post-qualification and advanced levels, she has worked as a social worker in field and residential settings in the statutory sector.

The State of Feminist Social Work

Vicky White

Routledge
Taylor & Francis Group

LONDON AND NEW YORK

First published 2006
by Routledge
2 Park Square, Milton Park, Abingdon, Oxon OX14 4RN

Simultaneously published in the USA and Canada
by Routledge
270 Madison Ave, New York, NY 10016

Routledge is an imprint of the Taylor & Francis Group, an informa business

© 2006 Vicky White

Typeset in Times
by Keystroke, 28 High Street, Tettenhall, Wolverhampton
Printed and bound in Great Britain
by The Cromwell Press, Trowbridge, Wiltshire

British Library Cataloguing in Publication Data
A catalogue record for this book is available from the British Library

Library of Congress Cataloging in Publication Data
A catalog record for this book has been requested

ISBN10: 0–415–32843–8 (hbk)
ISBN10: 0–415–32844–6 (pbk)
ISBN10: 0–203–96994–4 (ebk)

ISBN13: 978–0–415–32843–2 (hbk)
ISBN13: 978–0–415–32844–9 (pbk)
ISBN13: 978–0–203–96994–6 (ebk)

For John

Contents

Introduction

Any intellectual endeavour has a personal side, even if this is rarely articulated.
(Showstack-Sassoon 1987: 16)

A growing sense of unease

My interest in feminist social work can be traced to the late 1970s, when I was a trainee social worker in a Social Services Department. That interest developed further during my qualifying social work course at the beginning of the 1980s. As a trainee social worker and as a social work student, I read the limited amount of feminist social work literature that was available at the time, alongside being involved in feminist activism, some of which was within social work.

Post-qualification, my interest in feminist social work continued, as a residential social worker in a mental health setting. The staff team in this setting consisted, in the main, of a strong group of women (and two pro-feminist men) who shared a commitment to gendering mental health social work. We were keen to develop our understanding of women's mental health – of what were seen by male psychiatrists as women's illnesses – in an alternative direction. We regarded the women's 'problems' (always pronounced in the staff team with an ironic inflection) as a product of their experiences of societal oppression. We sought to develop an alternative stance to the medical model in an open way with women service users and this resulted in some blurring of roles between service users and staff. For example, in what now seems like a bygone age, during the residential social workers' dispute the service users actively supported intermittent strike action by staff, by undermining senior managers' attempts to maintain business as usual.

This commitment to gendering social work continued and broadened when I worked as a generic field social worker in a Social Services Department. In addition to undertaking individual casework in this setting, I worked with other women social workers to bring together women service users on the basis of a feminist understanding of how the personal difficulties they faced were generated in the public domain and could be addressed more collectively. Subsequently, as a hospital social worker and as a social worker in an adoption and fostering unit, my sense that gender was a significant dimension of social work was extended into other areas of practice.

Through the 1980s and into the 1990s, I read more feminist social work literature as it appeared. This literature provided accounts of how women's problems were constructed and critiqued their depiction in mainstream social work. However, attempting to move beyond feminist accounts and into being, as it were, an 'actually-existing-feminist-social-worker' in each of my jobs, proved to be more problematic than I anticipated. Overall, I was left with a feeling of unease about my credentials as a 'true' feminist social worker and a feeling of having failed to practice 'real' feminist social work on a consistent basis. This feeling has been captured by Wise:

> There are very many feminist practitioners in the field who have become guilty about not being able to live up to this Utopian vision of the empowering model of feminist social work, because the theory simply does not match the reality of their working lives . . . the empowerment model of feminist social work may be de-skilling and disempowering feminist and pro-feminist social workers: it sets them up to fail.
>
> (Wise 1995: 113)

We will return to the place of the empowerment model in the feminist social work literature later (see Chapter 2), but for now will remain with the feelings of unease and failure.

Failure or being failed?

I began to address these feelings of unease and failure and moved towards questioning the feminist social work literature, rather than myself, whilst undertaking a women's studies programme. I used my participation in the programme, in part, to re-read the feminist social work literature and to reconsider the ways in which feminist social workers related their experiences to that literature.

Re-reading the literature served to highlight the primacy accorded to feminist social work as an affiliation and alignment that was intended as the primary basis for a personal and political identity, seen as infusing the totality of the 'true' feminist social worker's practice. This explained the discomfort I experienced about whether I was a 'true' feminist social worker; there were times when I did not feel that I was immersed in a feminist identity. Feminism was not infusing my work in the all-encompassing sense conveyed by the literature. An alternative, and less self-blaming, way of putting this is that the feminist social work literature did not capture the tensions and ambiguities of my experiences or those of other women social workers to whom I talked. The more I went into this, the more the accounts of 'feminist social work' in the literature appeared to have been developed largely in the absence of consideration of the immediate experiences of women social workers like myself.

Following my completion of the women's studies programme, I was working in a university department and identified four particular points of tension between academic and experiential accounts of being a feminist social worker. First, as I have noted above, in the literature a woman social worker's feminist identity is taken as the given and unproblematic base from which to launch feminist social work. In contrast, women social workers' anecdotal accounts of their experiences were of feminist identities that were fluid, sometimes fragile or even non-existent. Such accounts were close to my own experience. Second, in the literature the identification of commonality of experiences between feminist social workers and women service users has been regarded as the basis upon which feminists can work non-hierarchically and non-oppressively with service users in egalitarian relationships. The direct experience of women social workers seemed to question the extent to which gender served as the basis for commonality of experiences and interests with women service users, as suggested by the literature, and questioned whether egalitarian relationships were feasible. Third, in the literature the goal of egalitarian relationships with women service users was expressed confidently as being concerned with their empowerment, whereas in practice there seemed to be a lack of clarity about what empowerment meant. Fourth, formulation of proposals for feminist social work in the literature tended to ignore or play down the impact of the statutory framework within which women social worker/women service user relationships were situated. Yet many women social workers seemed acutely conscious of encountering constraints when working in a statutory agency.

I decided to explore these tensions between the literature and practice by focusing on women social workers' experiences in statutory settings. This opened up the focus to constituencies of women who might understand their experiences in social work in ways other than those solely signified by 'feminist social work'. It allowed for 'diverse material realities . . . and the perspectives those realities generate' (Stanley and Wise 1990: 44) to be considered from a range of women's standpoints (Harding 1990: 96; 1991; Hill Collins 1991; Asfar and Maynard 1994; Stanley and Wise 1993). At the same time, it was an option that did not exclude any women social workers who might designate themselves as 'feminist social workers'.

In order to maximise the likelihood of the women social workers being those who were influenced by critical perspectives that encompassed addressing women's interests, I decided to invite participation from women social workers who had completed a practice teaching programme and who had a self-declared interest in women's perspectives on social work. Such participants would have been expected to consider gender issues as part of their practice teacher training. They would also have encountered relevant perspectives through their contact with social work courses subsequently and through having students with them on placement, as they reflected with students on the ways in which oppression was manifested in the work setting. In other words, a 'best case scenario' was being sought by inviting participation from women social workers who were interested in addressing women's interests in social work, had had the opportunity to have time out from their workplaces to reflect on perspectives which might inform addressing women's interests and were expected to continue exploring issues arising from those perspectives in their work with students.

The book explores the women social workers' accounts of their experiences against a backcloth of themes from the feminist social work literature and the context of state social work. Chapter 1 identifies a major theme in the feminist social work literature: calls to women social workers to align themselves with principles that have been proposed as the basis for feminist practice, and to embrace a feminist social work identity on the basis of those principles. Chapter 2 draws further themes out of the literature – the promotion of egalitarian relationships with women service users aimed at empowerment – and uncovers the neglect of the state context. The state context is then explored in Chapter 3 as being crucial to the development of an understanding of the characteristics and operation of social work. Specific developments in social work's organisational regimes, which culminated in the managerialism associated with the reform of social work, first under the Conservatives and then through New Labour, are discussed in Chapter 4. The changes to social work education, which have occurred in parallel with developments in social work's organisational regimes, are examined in Chapter 5. Of particular significance is the way in which social work education became a site on which issues of discrimination and oppression have been debated. In Chapter 6 attention shifts to the experiences of the women social workers. This chapter explores women social workers' accounts of their identities, identifications and stances, whilst Chapter 7 considers the extent to which they were able to pursue egalitarian relationships with women service users, with the goal of empowerment. Chapter 8 examines the women social workers' experiences of key aspects of managerial developments and Chapter 9 sets out their responses to those developments. The final chapter concludes with an assessment of the state of feminist social work and the prospects for addressing the interests of women social workers and service users.

Chapter 1

Feminist social work identity

Across 30 years of writing, a consistent emphasis in the feminist social work literature has been calls to women social workers to align themselves with principles that have been proposed as the basis for their practice. In seeing themselves as affiliated to what feminist social work is considered to stand for, women social workers have been urged to embrace a feminist social work identity that has been characterised as rooted in eclecticism. In the literature's elaboration of this eclecticism, it is common for the diverse perspectives that fed into the origins of feminist social work to be mentioned, with little precision about their legacies and a broad measure of consensus about the open-ended nature of feminist social work, rooted in common principles. This eclecticism has been reappraised because of the diversity that is concealed within the term 'women'. In response to critiques of eclecticism, one stance has been to view such challenges as capable of being used to revise and extend feminist social work, thus holding on to the promise of a unifying feminist identity. Another stance has been to seek to refine eclecticism through the adoption of a broader anti-discriminatory agenda that encompasses gender within a range of social divisions. Finally, some writers have stressed the splintering of feminist identity under the impact of postmodernist critique.

Eclecticism

Within much of the literature it is assumed that there is a feminist social work identity, readily accessible by women social workers, with which they can identify, align themselves and to which they can affiliate. For the most part, this remains an unstated assumption, serving as a foundation on which the literature's other themes are constructed. When this theme has surfaced explicitly, women social workers have often been seen as being totally immersed in their feminist social work identity. For example, Hudson *et al.* have stressed the 'feminist emphasis on the invariable influence of our values and how they inescapably permeate all that we do both professionally and personally' (Hudson *et al.* 1994: 96). Similarly, the Birmingham Women and Social Work Group held that feminism is both a personal and political commitment and that it cannot be utilised or discarded on a whim (Birmingham Women and Social Work Group 1985: 119).

Opening up access to the immersion of women social workers in this feminist social work identity has usually been undertaken in a particular way. It has been common for the diverse origins of feminist social work to be mentioned, with little precision about their legacies and a broad measure of consensus about the open-ended eclectic nature of feminist social work. For example, in an early example of this eclecticism, Hale acknowledged a broad range of feminist perspectives. She emphasised the common ground they shared, namely, 'consciousness of the inequality which women experience in relation to men and, resulting from this awareness, a desire to redress the balance and to remedy the injustices' (Hale 1984: 168). In similar vein, Dominelli and McLeod regarded feminist social work as being informed by Marxism, socialism and liberalism (Dominelli and McLeod 1989: 27). However, the contributions of these perspectives to the construction of feminist social work were seen as condensable into

> a very simple idea: that there are not two sorts of people in the world, the superior and the inferior, or in terms of power relations, the dominant and the subordinate. We are all equal irrespective of our gender. Social relations that obliterate this fact must therefore be transformed and recreated in ways that reflect equality in terms of gender.
>
> (Dominelli and McLeod 1989: 1)

Later, Dominelli extended the origins of feminist social work to liberal, radical, socialist and black feminisms. She concluded that these perspectives were united by their commitment to the elimination of gender inequality and saw them as having a set of five principles in common (Dominelli 1992: 85). These five principles are:

- the personal is political;
- egalitarian relations replacing hierarchy and inequality;
- the interconnectedness between different aspects of our lives and the interdependency between human beings;
- a dialectical relationship between theory and practice;
- social rights vested in a citizenship accruing to individuals by virtue of their existence rather than their social status – the 'I am, therefore, I have rights' principle.

> (Dominelli 1992: 86)

Elsewhere, Dominelli has stressed that liberal, radical, socialist, anti-racist and postmodernist feminisms have nine common characteristics that inform feminist social work's theory and practice, premised upon taking 'gendered inequality and its elimination as the starting point for working with women'. These nine characteristics are:

- upholding the right of women to be free from oppression;
- having women speak for themselves in their own voices;

- listening to what women have to say;
- creating alternative lifestyles in the here and now;
- integrating our theories with our practice;
- seeking compatibility between the ends being sought and the means whereby these are achieved;
- seeking collectivist solutions which respect the individuality and uniqueness of each woman;
- valuing women's contributions;
- using women's individual experiences to make sense of our social realities.

(Dominelli 2002a: 97)

These feminist principles and characteristics have been updated again by Dominelli, as 'relevant to practice and evident in feminist social work':

- recognising the diversity of women;
- valuing women's strengths;
- eliminating the privileging of certain groups of women to prevent difference from becoming a basis for unequal power relations between different groups of women;
- considering women as active agents capable of making decisions for themselves in all aspects of their lives;
- locating individual women in their social situations and acknowledging the interconnections between the individual and collective entities relevant to them;
- providing women with the space to voice their own needs and solutions to problems;
- acknowledging the principle 'the personal is political' is relevant at macro, meso and micro levels of practice;
- redefining private woes as public issues;
- ensuring that women's needs are addressed within the context of their being seen as whole human beings in which each area of life interacts with the others;
- recognising the interdependent nature of human relations and through that, realising that what happens to one individual or group has implications for everyone else;
- recognising that women's individual problems have social causes and addressing both levels in each intervention; and
- looking for collective solutions to individual problems.

(Dominelli 2002b: 162–163)

In arguing for a similarly eclectic approach[1] to the definition of feminist social work identity, Reynolds has suggested that liberal, radical and socialist feminisms cover a wide spectrum of debate but they share 'a questioning of notions that a woman's place is primarily in the home; that women should take the main responsibility for child-rearing; and that women are naturally suited to low-paid and low-status caring work' (Reynolds 1997: 74). She saw the eclectic approach as, what she terms, an 'evangelising' strategy:

> It is in the interests of the development of feminist practice to have as many women as possible thinking of themselves as feminists. This has led feminist social work academics to stress the breadth of possibilities offered by feminism: the common goals rather than the different purposes.
>
> (Reynolds 1997: 82)

This evangelising strategy was also evident in Hale's approach. In arguing for the common ground of feminist social work, she suggested that her earlier work could have appeared to be bland and impotent because it was deliberately designed to emphasise the unity of feminist stances so that those women who had not identified themselves with feminism as a political perspective, but who had some consciousness of women's inferior status and a desire to remedy it, would feel included in feminist social work (Hale 1984: 168). Similarly, McNay has suggested that feminist practitioners must show how their broad insights can be used by other workers who have yet to grasp the relevance of feminist analysis to the range of problems with which they are confronted (McNay 1992: 54).

Eclecticism reappraised

In its early days, the women's movement stressed the inequalities between women and men, later moving on to emphasise 'diversity *within* the concept of "woman", which for feminist analysis had previously been accepted as a unitary category' (Langan 1992a: 3–4, original emphasis). The consequences of diversity for feminist analysis have been depicted by some writers as far-reaching: 'An emphasis on difference has shattered the illusion of the homogeneity of, and sisterhood between, women, which previously characterised white, middle-class, Westernised feminist politics and analysis' (Asfar and Maynard 1994: 1). hooks has argued that 'The vision of sisterhood evoked by women liberationists was based on the idea of common oppression, a false and corrupt platform disguising and mystifying the true nature of women's varied and complex social reality' (hooks 1990: 29).

This general trend within feminism has been reflected in some of the feminist social work literature, although arguably to a less pronounced extent:

> Particular groups of women (for example, black women, lesbians and women with disabilities) have developed critiques of the ways in which they are dominated by other women, including feminists. Consequently, by the mid-1980s, it had become clear that feminism's presumption of 'universal sisterhood' was a conceptual and organisational barrier to addressing unequal relationships among women. The tendency of many recent feminist critiques of social work practice (my own included) has undoubtedly been to focus on the commonalties of women's experiences at the expense of recognising social

divisions that uphold the power of some groups of women at the expense of others.

(Hudson, A. 1989: 73)

From the late 1980s onwards, in addition to the overriding emphasis on an eclectic identity, forged in the fusion of a range of feminist perspectives, there were references to acknowledging differences amongst women (see, for example, Hanmer and Statham 1988: Ch. 1; Dominelli and McLeod 1989; Phillipson 1991: 17 and 38). Dominelli and McLeod, for example, highlighted critiques of feminism arising from the experiences women have from standpoints within a range of social divisions, such as class, 'race', sexuality, disability and age (Dominelli and McLeod 1989: 3–4). However, such references were seen as insufficient by some black, lesbian and disabled women who criticised the dominant feminist paradigm for its racism, ethnocentrism and heterosexism (Watson 1999: 4–5). The articulation of 'other voices' can be illustrated by drawing on examples in relation to 'race', disability and sexuality.

Black women's lives, and the specificity of their experiences, were regarded as remaining invisible or being distorted so that they fitted into a white mould (Carby 1982; Bryan *et al.* 1985; Ramazanoglu 1986). These critiques were incorporated into social work (see, for example, Shah 1989; Watt and Cooke 1989; Lewis 1996):

> When white women write about women they often write only about themselves. When they occasionally write about black women they usually just incorporate them in a racist and ethnocentric way . . . white women have made black women mere appendages to the perspectives of white feminists.
>
> (Shah 1989: 178)

This incorporation of black women led Watt and Cooke to argue that it is the experience of racism that is the crucial division between black and white women. Black women share this experience with black men and, in spite of their oppression by men, they argued that it was racism that should remain a priority on the social work agenda (Watt and Cooke 1989: 75).

Another strand of critique came from women with disabilities who challenged their marginalisation and exclusion (Morris 1991/1992, 1993, 1996; Begum 1994, 1995), and other women commentators (see, for example, Fawcett 1998, 2000). Such writers highlighted the importance of bringing disabled women's perspectives into social work: 'When we appear as a public issue it is usually in the way the non-disabled world defines us and our concerns and not in a way we wish to appear ourselves' (Morris 1993: 124). Begum insisted that disability, whilst needing to be given greater prominence, should not be regarded in isolation from the experience of other social divisions and argued that the way disabilities are perceived and experienced is determined by the way they interconnect with dimensions of 'race', gender, sexuality, class and age (Begum 1994: 21). She argued that black disabled women do not experience forms of oppression separately or in a hierarchical structure and should not be asked to compartmentalise their experiences into discrete categories (Begum 1994: 18).

In relation to sexuality, Cosis-Brown maintained that the feminist social work literature had little, beyond generalities, to say about being lesbians (Cosis-Brown 1992: 204; 1998). She argued that lesbian social workers are either ignored or seen solely in relation to their sexual orientation (Cosis-Brown 1992: 9). She queried this simplistic view of sexuality and suggested that self-definition as lesbian is an ongoing series of difficult processes, which is different for different women (Cosis-Brown 1992: 202). Hillin considered that part of these difficult processes is that some lesbian social workers still feel very vulnerable about coming out in social work settings and, as a consequence, are continually on guard to avoid giving anything away which might reveal their sexuality (Hillin 1985: 18). Black lesbian social workers encounter even more pressures within social work organisations: 'Black women may not identify as lesbians in certain situations, making a rational choice about not wanting to take on racism and homophobia at the same time' (Cosis-Brown 1992: 202).

The reappraisal of eclecticism is summed up in Ang's assertion that feminism

> can never ever be an encompassing home for all women, not just because different groups of women have different and sometimes conflicting interests, but, more radically, because for many groups of 'other' women other interests, other identifications are sometimes more important and politically pressing than, or even incompatible with, those related to their being women.
>
> (Ang 1995: 73)

In the feminist social work literature, the difficulties that emerged from the articulation of diversity and difference were addressed largely through the refinement of eclecticism.

Eclecticism refined

In response to critiques of eclecticism, one stance taken in the feminist social work literature has been to view such challenges as capable of being used to revise and extend feminist social work identity (Dominelli and McLeod 1989: 2–3). Through this process of refinement, it has been argued, critiques that reflect social divisions other than gender can be identified with feminist social work:

> A feminist stance endorses egalitarianism across all social dimensions. Therefore, feminists are also against other social divisions which reflect dominance and subordination such as race, class, heterosexism, ageism and 'ablebodiedism' . . . feminist responses to criticism of their theory and practice is sufficiently advanced to demonstrate that incorporated as a central feature

of a feminist stance on social inequality is the rejection of all social divisions and not simply those based on gender.

(Dominelli and McLeod 1989: 2 and 4)

This elaboration of feminist social work's identity has been indicated by Dominelli through extensions to its terminology, for example, 'anti-racist feminist social work' (Dominelli 1991), 'anti-racist socialist feminist social work' (Dominelli 1992), 'anti-racist feminist sociological social work' (Dominelli 1997).

Thus, the inclusion of different women's experiences and standpoints has not necessarily been seen as undermining the unifying identity that has emerged from the feminist social work agenda: 'Unity-diversity . . . encourages us to respect difference, preserve uniqueness, while also seeing similarities and wholeness' (Phillipson 1991: 18). There has been a sense of confidence that routes through to an eclectic identity could still be found. In relation to 'race', for example, feminist social work writers have acknowledged that although black and white women have considerable differences to contend with between them, they are also grappling with common causes, and the principle of sisterhood need not be lost (Dominelli and McLeod 1989: 30). A refined eclecticism has been seen as still offering the basis for feminist social work:

There are a number of principles that feminists share, regardless of their overall analyses and calls for action. These include integrating the personal and political dimensions of life, respecting the diversity encompassed by women, seeking more egalitarian forms of social relationships and transforming the existing social order . . . Women have persevered in searching for ways of symbolically and practically emphasising their commitment to 'unity in diversity'.

(Dominelli 2002b: 3–4)

The emergence of a diverse range of women's standpoints on to the feminist social work agenda has often been discussed in this way; in terms of how differences amongst women can be incorporated into feminist practice and ultimately transcended. Thus Cavanagh and Cree have suggested that although a single feminist standpoint cannot adequately express the reality of women's lives, women still have common experience and common goals (Cavanagh and Cree 1996: xxi). Hanmer and Statham saw this recognition of commonality as the cornerstone of feminist social work and stressed that recognition of diversity occurs in the context of commonality (Hanmer and Statham 1999: 19). Hudson *et al.* warned that, as a result of this tendency towards stressing commonality of identity, feminist social work had been castigated for being synonymous with the values and experiences of white, heterosexual middle-class women (Hudson *et al.* 1994: 9) and Graham concluded that 'feminist social work has yet to engage in a systematic way with the debates about difference and divisions among women . . . masking "race", class, sexuality and disability as crucial dimensions of women's lives'

(Graham 1992: 63). Despite such earlier cautions, the promise of a unifying feminist identity remains a theme in some of the literature.

Identity diversified

In contrast to attempts in the feminist social work literature to refine eclecticism and rescue a unifying feminist identity, Langan has sought the kind of engagement that Graham saw as having been lacking. Langan began by identifying the need to move beyond the limitations of the past in feminist social work through attempting to develop a wider, non-oppressive, anti-discriminatory form of social work theory and practice that recognised the complexity and diversity of the oppressions that affect women's lives (Langan 1992a: 1). Rather than seeing feminist social work as capable of expanding its eclecticism to incorporate challenges from a range of oppressions, Langan argued for the necessity of constructing an anti-discriminatory social work from the

> growing recognition of the specificities of oppression according to gender, race, class, age, disability and sexual orientation. [Anti-discriminatory social work] emphasises the diversity of experience and the validity of each person's experience. It seeks to develop an understanding of both the totality of oppression and its specific manifestations as the precondition for developing an anti-discriminatory practice relevant to all spheres of social work.
>
> (Langan 1992a: 3)

Similarly, Hudson, in acknowledging that the pursuit of greater gender equality has sometimes been at the expense of recognising other oppressions (particularly those experienced by black, lesbian and working-class women), regarded the dynamics and effects of oppression as kaleidoscopic configurations of relationships between different forms of oppression that are constantly moving and changing (Hudson, A. 1989: 93). Wise also reached the conclusion that the development of anti-discriminatory social work, informed not only by feminist analysis but also drawing on the analyses of other subjugated groups, needed to be the priority (Wise 1995: 113).

Having identified some of the challenges to the construction of a feminist social work identity, we now turn to what is potentially a more fundamental challenge; that posed by the emergence of postmodernist perspectives that have cut across and through discussions of social divisions in social work (see, for example, Sands and Nuccio 1992; Williams 1996; Parton and Marshall 1998; Pease and Fook 1999; Fawcett et al. 2000; Healy 1999, 2000, 2005).

Identity splintered

Healy maintains that 'since the 1990s, postmodern theories have had a growing influence on the formal base of social work and have contributed to new theories for social work practice' (Healy 2005: 193). In relation to feminist perspectives more generally, postmodernism has been regarded by some writers as embodying a major criticism of feminist adherence to 'grand theories'. The implication is that whilst postmodernism does not result in a narrative that subsumes women, neither does it privilege feminist narratives which would accord primacy to women's oppression (Evans 1995: 125). For this reason, Dominelli has adopted a critical stance towards postmodernism's influence on social work:

> . . . postmodern social work has yet to establish itself as a credible base for practice . . . Postmodern social work is likely to be more individualistic than a feminist one with its commitment to collective solutions and approaches to problems, even when delivering services to an individual. Postmodern and feminist approaches do not sit well together.
>
> (Dominelli 2002b: 56–57)

Other writers have welcomed postmodernism's emphasis on diffuse power, diversity and difference and seen it as having the potential to contribute to feminist social work through its support for competing discourses around being a woman. (See, for example, Featherstone and Fawcett's discussion [1995a] of child sexual abuse; Fawcett's case study of disability [1998, 2000]; Taylor and White's use of discourse analytic tools to examine child abuse and mental health practice [2000] and Milner's use of narrative and solution-focused work with women [2001]). In particular, postmodernism has questioned approaches that present either power or difference as fixed, clear-cut categories (Featherstone and Fawcett 1995b). Work on difference has attempted to move feminist social work away from universalist perspectives and towards seeing diversity as a resource rather than an obstacle. Accordingly, feminist social workers have been encouraged to 'recognise and work with the ways in which they are divided as well as the ways in which they are united' (Featherstone and Fawcett 1995c: 9). Featherstone and Fawcett have been sceptical of theories that put forward insufficiently self-critical universal explanations and have argued for theoretical work aimed at identifying specific effects of oppression rather than 'grand causes' (Featherstone and Fawcett 1995a: 64):

> Critique of the tyranny and imperialism of grand theories, which try and impose order on complex phenomena, can help validate those who stress the complexity and ambiguity of people's lives. As Fraser and Nicholson (1990) argue, this does not mean abandoning large-scale analyses completely . . . analyses must be historically, temporally and culturally specific, and comparative rather than universalist.
>
> (Featherstone and Fawcett 1995a: 36)

The importance accorded to difference by postmodernism has been seen by some writers as fragmenting feminist social work's foundation in an identity built on eclecticism (see, for example, Dominelli 1997: 39–40; Dominelli 2002b: 57). Whilst acknowledging the significant differences that exist between women, Hallett nevertheless has argued that gender is still a crucial dimension and that the position of women should be central to the analysis of social work, with women's needs and capacities at the forefront of planning and service delivery (Hallett 1989: xi–xii). Hallett has also regarded the postmodernist recognition and celebration of diversity and difference, locality and specificity, as serving to obscure the structural position of women (Hallett 1996: 10).

The challenges from the critiques of feminist social work have raised questions about whether and, if so, how, the category of 'woman' should be retained. Drawing on Stanley (1990), Orme has argued that

> not all women share the same state of being, nor does the state of being exist in relation to something essentially female, but to the social construction of 'women'. This construction, and the oppressions identified within the construction, recognises many forms of women's existence or condition which are incorporated in it . . . thus allowing for the separate and different experiences of black women, lesbian women, disabled women and older women, for example.
>
> (Orme 1998: 226)

Similarly, Langan's concern has been that recognising diversity among women should not detract from recognising the concept of 'woman' and the imbalance in power between women and men. However, she has argued that the stress on diversity involves challenging the nature of power, whoever holds it (Langan 1992a: 5).

Stanley has suggested that terms like 'women', 'feminism' and 'gender' are constructed in particular ways by women. Some women use them strategically, some women use them accidentally, whilst for others they are an indication of political and analytical intention. Stanley adds a note of caution about such categorisation: 'It should be recognised that a variety of terminological usages co-exist, sometimes indicating deep conceptual and political difference and disagreement, sometimes indicating nothing so much as casual choice' (Stanley 1997: 11). Notwithstanding her note of caution, Stanley suggests that terminology can help to identify different women's standpoints. A similar approach is taken by Reynolds who maintains that gender, feminism and women's experiences are interwoven for many feminists and that there may be strategic reasons for choosing one term rather than another (Reynolds 1994: 8).

Conclusion

The dominant view in the feminist social work literature has been that women social workers can align themselves with and affiliate to an all-embracing eclectic feminist identity as a standpoint from which to approach their work. This dominant view has been questioned by writers who have emphasised the existence of diverse identities amongst women. Such writers have suggested that women's identities are not necessarily coterminous with feminist social work. Women social workers may, instead, locate themselves within a more loosely defined stance of anti-discriminatory practice, although this does not necessarily preclude a focus on women. Postmodernist critique has splintered feminist identity by seeking to shift feminist social work away from universalist perspectives and towards seeing diversity as a resource to be celebrated. The existence of diverse and splintered identities amongst women has raised the question as to whether women social workers can align themselves with an all-embracing feminist identity as a stance from which to approach their work. Feminist social work identity, rooted in eclecticism, has been the basis in the literature for the advocacy of egalitarian relationships and empowerment, to which Chapter 2 now turns.

Chapter 2

Egalitarian relationships, empowerment and statutory social work

The previous chapter explored the feminist social work literature's proposal that women social workers can adopt a feminist identity as the basis for their practice and reviewed perspectives that have questioned this proposal. The literature has suggested that this feminist social work identity should be geared towards establishing egalitarian relationships between women social workers and women service users, with the goal of empowerment. Some writers have queried the sustainability of this position because they have regarded it as not grounded in the realities of practice in the statutory context.

Egalitarian relationships

Most of the feminist social work texts have emphasised the extent to which social work consists of women working with women (for example, Brook and Davies 1985a: 143; Dominelli and McLeod 1989: 15, 106–107; Hallett 1989: ix, Ch.1; Dominelli 1991: 197; 1997: 85; 2002a: 97; Hanmer and Statham 1999: 3, 99–100; Reynolds 1997: 74; Orme 1998: 218): 'Where state welfare services intervene in the personal and social problems individuals and families experience, it is mainly with and through women, as its agents, ministering to other women' (Davis and Brook 1985: 4). Even when there are male service users in the picture, it has been noted that it is usually a woman who is the main or only focus of social work intervention (Hale 1984: 167; Hudson, A. 1989: 78; Humphreys 1994).

This woman-to-woman relationship in social work has been the starting point for the most consistently advocated theme in the feminist social work literature: that a central task of feminist social workers is to create egalitarian relationships with women service users. Such relationships have been regarded as containing strong elements of recognition, mutuality and reciprocity on the basis of a shared experience of oppression. Dominelli has suggested that

> Despite the problematics of practising feminist social work, working with service users in more egalitarian ways is a promising avenue to walk down because it offers the opportunity to: explore power-sharing, learn how to dismantle the barriers to egalitarian social relations; build the bridge necessary

for surmounting these obstacles; transcend the false-equality traps that fail to resolve a myriad of problems; value difference; and create alternative ways of being.

(Dominelli 2002b: 83)

Feminist social work has been viewed as prefiguring the egalitarian forms of practice towards which feminism in general has been regarded as striving, and as demonstrating that it is possible to develop such prefigurative forms (Dominelli 1992: 95), if social workers seek to minimise power differentials between themselves and service users (Dominelli 2002b: 39).

Accordingly, feminist social workers have been exhorted to see the main relevance of gender to social work as being this focus on women (Hanmer and Statham 1999: 1). For example, the ethos of the relationship Hanmer and Statham have proposed is

To value women, to utilise their strengths and abilities as a resource . . . Women social workers need to spend time with women talking about issues and experiences that are important to women. This can be an enjoyable time from which social workers as well as clients can gain a feeling of exhilaration. It can be a time in which information is exchanged about ways social workers work, about support systems, about ways of dealing with men. Clients can be accepted as competent, as having strengths and rights.

(Hanmer and Statham 1999: 127)

Women social workers have been urged to use such working relationships with women service users as the basis for developing women-centred practice, geared to what women want and need (Phillipson 1991). Such practice is seen as respecting and valuing women (Dominelli, 1997: 28), affirming the specificity of women's experiences (Hudson, A. 1989: 73; Dominelli 1998a: 918) and making women visible in their own right (Hanmer and Statham 1999: 57).

In recognising the importance of the woman-to-woman process of feminist social work (Dominelli 1997: 28), the existence of commonality has been a central point of emphasis of the feminist social work literature. As we saw in Chapter 1, the feminist social work literature has placed considerable emphasis on eclecticism, rooted in commonality of experience, as the basis for women social workers immersing themselves in feminist social work identity. Commonality has been seen not only as the source of identity but also as the basis on which relationships between women social workers and women service users can be built, with the objective of promoting egalitarian relationships (Marchant and Wearing 1986: 61; Dominelli and McLeod 1989: 22; Dominelli 2002b: 9). Phillipson has argued that the mutuality of this woman-to-woman social work relationship should be valued as much as the completion of specific tasks (Phillipson 1991: 71). The process of social work – the ways in which services are offered and the experience of women working together – has been seen as the hallmark of feminism and as more important than either the services themselves or the meeting of objectives (Orme 1998: 223–224; Dominelli 2002a: 98; 2002b: 77).

The egalitarian relationships between women social workers and women service users have been seen as rooted in their common experiences of oppression. Early on in the development of the feminist social work literature, Wilson observed that women social workers are probably the only group who share a similar experience of oppression with many of their clients (Wilson 1975: 31) and Kravetz suggested that women social workers should recognise their unity with women clients (Kravetz 1976: 167). Some years later the Birmingham Women and Social Work Group noted that as women they had experiences in common which could be shared and explored with women service users (Birmingham Women and Social Work Group 1985: 119) and Hanmer and Statham have suggested that

> Within the complex and changing forms of service delivery, women social workers and clients continue to share commonalties. They group around being female, their relationships with men, children, living within the family, employment and working conditions, and more general cultural expectations and pressures on women. These commonalties offer both a resource and a strength for practice. We suggest that it is only through a recognition of commonalties that a true assessment of the situation facing women clients and a user-centred practice can emerge.
>
> (Hanmer and Statham 1999: 18)

Leaving aside the heterosexual assumption about the basis for commonality in this statement, and the assumption of homogeneity in heterosexual family forms, Hanmer and Statham's argument is that the needs of women cannot be assessed until social workers become aware of the commonalties between their lives and those of women service users. They identify these commonalties as: the problematic impact on women of female life experience; the public–private division of life through managing the double load of home and paid work; women's relationships with men and their impact on women's private and public worlds; being mothers and caring for dependants generally; women's relationships with women; the influence more generally of society on women (Hanmer and Statham 1999: 10). They have argued that these commonalties exist

> between women irrespective of age, life-stage, sexuality, class, race, reproductive history . . . In making the commonalties we share as women conscious, visible parts of our practice we learn that we need not, and indeed must not, be ashamed or surprised by them but incorporate them into our work.
>
> (Hanmer and Statham 1999: 10–11)

In this vein, Dominelli and McLeod have gone further than most writers in moving beyond commonality of experience as the basis for feminist social work and on to stressing the importance of the common material interests between women social workers and women service users (Dominelli and McLeod 1989: 147).

The emphasis placed on commonality of experience and common material interests has led to calls for feminist social workers to develop relationships with women service users that are built on equality, trust and sharing (Hanmer and Statham 1999: 142). Marchant and Wearing have suggested that this can be accomplished through the creation of equal relationships that demystify the social work role (Marchant and Wearing 1986: 5) and Fook proposed that one way in which this sort of relationship can be achieved is by relocating the venue for interviews and conducting them in the park, over lunch, or whilst doing the supermarket shopping (Fook 1986: 56).

Postmodernist perspectives, whilst having much more of an emphasis on difference (see Chapter 1), have produced remarkably similar prescriptions for the process of social work:

> It is thus essential for practitioners . . . [to] construct through dialogue with the client, a shared understanding and reality which they agree is a representation of their interaction . . . The creative capacities of the social worker must be understood . . . as a co-creator of harmony, particularly with those who are marginalised and excluded . . . In social work encounters, solutions are not as much arrived at but found in the making, the telling and the talking.
> (Parton and Marshall 1998: 246–248)

Using such perspectives in relation to feminist social work, Featherstone and Fawcett have called for collaborative methods of interpreting meaning and engaging in dialogue around the meanings attached to needs, rights and responsibilities, which form the basis of most social worker/service user relationships (Featherstone and Fawcett 1995b: 14).

This stress on egalitarian relationships, with women social workers working with women service users on the basis of commonality, has been seen as having a range of implications in the feminist social work literature.

First, social problems have to be redefined from a feminist perspective by considering all problems in terms of their specific impact on women's welfare. This requires an examination of problems from the starting point of women's experiences of them (Dominelli and McLeod 1989: 22), with the most fundamental precept being to believe the woman, to accept her and the problem she brings (Hanmer and Statham 1999: 141).

Second, as far as assessment is concerned, this should be focused on redefining the problem(s) from a feminist perspective:

> [feminist social work's] immediate aim is to use helping relationships predicated on egalitarian values . . . a facilitating relationship encourages the woman to make her own decisions by playing an active role in assessing her situation, exploring alternatives, formulating plans of action and implementing

them. The assessment process is likely to involve redefining the problem being considered from a feminist perspective. This removes it from the private realm of a personal problem for which the woman is solely responsible and lodges it in the public domain as a social problem which she is experiencing individually along with a number of other women.

(Dominelli 1997: 246)

Third, as we have already seen, the process of the social work relationship has been regarded as just as important as its goal(s):

Both the ends and means are imbued with egalitarian principles . . . For feminists, the process whereby needs are met is as important as the ends being sought . . . The exchange process must reflect the egalitarian relationships embodied in the service that is made available and requires the full involvement of both users and workers in the creation of that service. In other words, feminist social work is about creating non-exploitative egalitarian relationships aimed at promoting individual well-being through collective means available to all at point of need.

(Dominelli 1992: 87–88)

Whilst not discounting some of the positive potential inherent in woman-to-woman working relationships, the feminist social work literature's emphasis on women social workers and women service users engaging in egalitarian relationships can also be seen as problematic.

To begin with, the stress on commonality of experience suggests a tendency to regard women as a homogeneous group. As we saw in Chapter 1, an emphasis on homogeneity sidesteps, and as a consequence obscures, the different experiences and standpoints among women and the significance of other social divisions in upholding the power of some groups of women at the expense of others (Hudson, A. 1989: 72; Langan 1992a).

Further, focusing so heavily on the presumption of an inherent mutuality in the relationships between women social workers and women service users runs the risk of suggesting, if only by implication, that women working with women defines what feminism means in social work. If that were the case, to work solely or predominantly with women could be seen as unwittingly reinforcing notions of women as the source of, and solution to, the problems presented to social workers (see Milner 1993, 2001). Cavanagh and Cree, for example, comment that although feminism has in their view rightly placed women at the centre of social work, it has also provided a rationale for opting out of work with male service users, with the possibility that men's behaviour may go unchecked and that stereotypes about women's caring role in the family and within the social welfare network may be reinforced (Cavanagh and Cree 1996: 6).

A final consequence of the literature's focus on commonality has been that differences of interest between women social workers and women service users, stemming from the nature of the power relationship (see the section on the statutory context page 25), are obscured or wished away. The problematic nature of this position can be illustrated through the use of a number of examples from the feminist social work literature.

In arguing for equality in women social worker/women service user encounters, the Birmingham Women and Social Work Group stated that a feminist principle is that women social workers should not ask more of women service users than they ask of themselves (Birmingham Women and Social Work Group 1985: 121). This suggestion in itself demonstrates the nature of the power relationship: women social workers are in a position to make demands on ('to ask of') women service users, if they choose to do so.[1] Tucked into a statement by Dominelli and McLeod is another glimpse of what the reality of the woman social worker/woman service user relationship might be like:

> Complementing and indissolubly fused with feminism's egalitarian stance on welfare is its concern to engage in egalitarian practice related to its aims. We would argue that this has been the hallmark of feminist action in whatever sphere since the emergence of the contemporary women's movement. Again the idea at the heart of it is a simple one. If feminists aim to create egalitarian social relations then these must be reflected in their practice, otherwise it contradicts feminist aims and whatever social relations are being created they are not feminist ones.
>
> (Dominelli and McLeod 1989: 8–9)

This quotation indicates that the feminist social worker is introducing 'aims' into the encounter with the woman service user from the outset and is in a position to be able to do so, as Hale makes clear in this example:

> The file was read by the author . . . and Margaret was approached with the stance, maintained throughout contact with her, that she had been the victim of a restrictive upbringing related to her gender and that the early years of her adult life represented a search for loving stable relationships and a secure home.
>
> (Hale 1984: 172)

In the following quotation, whilst Dominelli and McLeod point to the shift in the nature of the power relations feminist social workers should seek to achieve, it is premised upon a prior shift by the feminist social worker of the account of the problem, indicating some of the power she possesses in problem definition:

> . . . the processes whereby problem definition itself occurs need to be carried out in an egalitarian way in order to foster the egalitarian relations that are being sought. This has brought about a critical shift in the nature of the power relations surrounding such work, a shift away from both 'psychopathologising'

the origins of 'individual' problems and accepting the appropriateness of placing the analysis of the social origins of individual misery and the right of the oppressed to speak for themselves.

(Dominelli and McLeod 1989: 32)

Finally, the Birmingham Women and Social Work Group, whilst supporting commonality of oppression and experience, point to divergent material interests with the women service users with whom they work:

The values and ideas that come from our feminism also suggest ways in which we can work from within existing state institutions for different forms of social relationships in order to provide a basis for new kinds of relationships with the recipients of our service . . . While we can use our feminism as a direct approach to women, it would clearly be naive to claim immediate and unconditional rapport with all women on the basis of our common experience of living in a male dominated world. We acknowledge as mainly white, middle-class, salaried women we are distanced from many of our clients.

(Birmingham Women and Social Work Group 1985: 118–120)

Wise has gone beyond these glimpses of problematic aspects of commonality and has provided a thoroughgoing consideration of feminist social work in which she maintained that the principles for practice identified by most feminist writers are not sustainable, particularly as far as the pursuit of egalitarian relationships is concerned. She saw feminism and statutory social work as antithetical. She unravelled the problematic nature of creating feminist social work practice in statutory settings and argued that the issue of power in social work, which has been glimpsed through scrutinising some of the quotations given above, has tended to be overlooked. The gist of Wise's argument was that feminist social work is a particular form of practice that came out of the political and social movements of 'second wave' feminism in the 1970s and 1980s. She has suggested that feminist social work practice cannot be transplanted to a statutory framework that is essentially antithetical to its policies and goals, but should instead be encouraged to develop separately. As we saw in the previous chapter, Wise has regarded the development of a broader anti-discriminatory approach to social work as being a feasible alternative to feminist social work, with the aim of not creating, supporting or adding to (rather than trying to eliminate) discrimination and oppression. Thus, rather than continuing to use the term 'feminist social work' in statutory settings, she has argued that it should only be retained for alternative services for women (Wise 1995: 113). Similarly, Orme has questioned 'whether social work, or more specifically statutory social work, could be "for women"' (Orme 2003: 133). Although she has regarded the reconciliation of the personal and the political within statutory social work as a major tension, she has concluded that the challenge is to theorise the feminine in ways that are not oppressive and to influence social work practice in ways that are liberatory (ibid. 134). The emphasis on the liberatory potential of feminist social work has been most prevalent in discussions of the goal of empowerment.

Empowerment

Chambon has commented that 'one way to reflect upon the signs of change occurring in a profession or academic field is to examine the language of professional claims' (cited in Pease 2002: 135). During the 1990s, 'empowerment' was a term that began to 'trip lightly off the tongue' in social work (Ward and Mullender 1991: 22). It is a term that has been imbued with a range of meanings:

> For some, such as Ward and Mullender (1991) and Langan and Lee (1989) for example, the idea of empowerment is inextricably linked with the wider struggle against an oppressive and 'disempowering' professional practice; for others, such as the purchasers and providers of health and social care services, its use more commonly serves as a synonym for 'enabling' users to have their say about the services they receive. Moreover, the idea of empowerment has found a place in a wide spectrum of political and ideological positions. On the one hand, for example, it plays a central role in the discourse of service user groups or 'new social welfare movements' (Williams 1992), who are pressing for more control over the services they receive; on the other, it has a key place in the literature of the New Right theorists of the welfare market, concerned with freeing the individual from unnecessary interference by, or dependence upon, those services.
>
> (Lupton 1998: 107)

Given the availability of this range of meanings, how has empowerment been construed within the feminist social work literature?

Empowerment was not mentioned by contributors to the literature on feminist social work in the 1970s and 1980s, with the exception of Comley who referred to empowerment in terms of addressing the imbalance of power between service users and social workers and as being the first step towards transforming the experience of welfare (Comley 1989: 67). From the 1990s onwards, however, feminist social work writing began referring to empowerment (see, for example, Ward and Mullender 1991; Langan and Day 1992; Dominelli 1992, 1997, 2002a, 2002b; Hudson *et al.* 1994; Wise 1995; Cavanagh and Cree 1996; Lupton 1998; Orme 1998 and 2001; Cohen and Mullender 2003). Dominelli's work provides an example of the approach that has been adopted in these texts. She regarded empowerment as the means of shaking off the shackles of social work:

> Feminists have . . . extended the concept of empowerment. Whilst the practice of feminist ideals may be somewhat imperfect because feminists have like other members of society internalised its social divisions, and they have to operate from within its hierarchical structures, they are none the less formally

committed to shedding these restraints and operating without them in their current work.

(Dominelli 1992: 98)

In particular, Dominelli argued that the feminist redefinition of a woman service user's problems, discussed in the previous section, is empowering for her because her experience is validated and her questioning of her position is one form of resistance, leading to her gaining greater control over her life (Dominelli 2002a: 98; and see Orme 1998: 221, 227). Elsewhere, Dominelli identified social work as being concerned with the individual and collective empowerment of service users, as opposed to its being a means of controlling women, with empowerment in service user–social worker relationships serving as a strategy for change (Dominelli 1997: 1, 223), a theme to which she has returned subsequently: 'Feminist social workers aim to promote the capabilities of women workers and "clients" to become full citizens capable of taking control of their lives within empowering social contexts' (Dominelli 2002b: 38).

It has been argued that groupwork provides one of the means by which empowerment of women can be achieved: 'Feminism and groupwork have always found a natural home together in empowerment agendas' (Cohen and Mullender 2003: 9). Cohen and Mullender have suggested that lessons can be learned from the empowerment potential in Ward and Mullender's 'self-directed groupwork' (1991), which 'heard silenced voices, and worked jointly and reflexively with service users in ways that did not privilege professional knowledge' (Cohen and Mullender 2003: 10). A collection of contributions contained in *Women, Oppression and Social Work* (Langan and Day 1992) broadens out empowerment into a number of fields, for example in relation to 'modes of intervention' (McNay 1992), in work with black single mothers (Bryan 1992), in residential care (Aymer 1992) and with older women (Hughes and Mtezuka 1992).

For the most part, then, 'empowerment' has been seen as a useful addition to the feminist social work vocabulary and to the strategy to be pursued through more egalitarian relationships with women service users. Langan, however, has questioned the usefulness of empowerment and sees it as having come to refer to an individualistic conception of power which reduces social relationships to the interpersonal level and obscures wider power relations in society, leaving coping and survival as its limited objectives. As such she has seen empowerment as typified by inviting service users to participate in decisions over which they have no control and as reconciling people to being powerless (Langan 1998: 214–215; and see, Humphries 1997). Forrest has maintained that

Empowerment is a force for both change and control. On the one hand, it is a social force which can generate social movement. It is a concept which gives meaning to a challenge to the status quo. Equally, it is a concept which obfuscates reality – it hides professional, managerial and political control.

(Forrest 2000: 8)

The individualistic conception of empowerment, highlighted by Langan, has been evident in definitions that have been employed in texts promoting anti-discriminatory practice, even when these definitions are expressed forcefully, for example:

> [Empowerment involves] enabling people who are disempowered to have more control over their own lives, to have a greater voice in institutions, services and situations which affect them, and to exercise power over someone else rather than simply being the recipients of exercised power.
>
> (Braye and Preston-Shoot 1995: 48)

Wise has provided a substantial critique of what she refers to as 'the ethic of empowerment' in the feminist social work literature (Wise 1995). She observed that ideas about empowerment in feminist social work have been drawn from models of facilitated or autonomous forms of women's self-help, such as rape crisis centres and women's refuges, which are feminist alternatives, deliberately constructed outside mainstream social work (Wise 1995: 110). This derivation of the model of empowerment in feminist social work is acknowledged by a number of writers (see, for example, Davis and Brook 1985: 5; Hudson 1985: 635–636; 1989: 71; Dominelli and McLeod 1989: 1; Dominelli 1992: 85, 99, 101; Dominelli 2002a: 97): 'Our starting point is that the most developed forms of feminist social work have taken place outside statutory social work . . . For statutory social work to become truly feminist it needs to embody such egalitarian initiatives within its practice' (Dominelli and McLeod 1989: 160).

As we have seen, Wise has argued that this transposition of feminist social work from contexts controlled by women into the (supposedly) egalitarian relationships between women social workers and women service users in statutory social work, in the belief that the woman service user will then be empowered, is unachievable (Wise 1995: 106–107). She has pointed out that these statutory-based relationships are artificially created and contain an imbalance of power, which is the missing dimension in feminist social work's analysis of statutory settings. Accordingly, she claims that feminist social work's 'universalised concept of empowerment' is not grounded in the realities of practice in the statutory context (Wise 1995: 111).

The statutory context

In Chapter 1, we saw how the feminist social work literature has laid strong emphasis on women social workers embracing a feminist identity and in the previous sections of this chapter we have seen how this has been regarded as the basis for forging egalitarian relationships with women service users, with the goal of empowerment. The backcloth to the discussion of these themes has been the statutory context, which has only been acknowledged in passing thus far but is now brought into the foreground.

Accounts of the impact of feminist social work in statutory settings have reached varying conclusions. Over the years, some writers have regarded the impact of feminist social work as being modest: it has had a 'marginal effect' (Hudson 1985: 635); 'had little impact' (Dominelli 1992: 83); has been a 'minority activity' (Dominelli and McLeod 1989: 125) and has had a 'lack of appeal as a major method of intervention in statutory social work' (Dominelli 2002b: 76). Others are more optimistic: feminist social work placed gender 'on the social work map' and had a 'profound effect on social work practice' (Dominelli 2002a: 99–100); it has gained a 'strong foothold' (Dominelli 1997: 42–43); it has made a 'significant contribution' (Dominelli and McLeod 1989: 10; and see Dominelli 1997: 104); and has 'an identifiable, extensive and widespread programme of action' (Dominelli and McLeod 1989: 114). Orme has concluded that the 'feminist analysis of child abuse and violence is perhaps the most well developed area but writers have explicitly used feminist theory to explore the experiences of other user groups' (Orme 2003: 132). Faced with the wide-scale changes in social work that began with Thatcherism (see Chapter 4), Dominelli was optimistic about the impact that feminist social work would continue to have on future developments because of the presence of practising feminist social workers within state welfare provision, the voluntary sector and commercial services (Dominelli 1992: 101).

For Cavanagh and Cree, feminist practitioners remained one of the energising forces in a profession that was becoming increasingly competence-driven and dominated by management and market ideologies (Cavanagh and Cree 1996: 182). Cree has concluded:

> While the more extensive claims of feminism may have been relegated to the margins, there is undoubtedly a level at which the general aims of anti-discriminatory and anti-sexist agenda have become accepted within the social work enterprise. There are also specific instances of a feminist approach becoming 'mainstreamed', for example, in criminal justice work with violent offenders.
>
> (Cree 2001: 156)

Within the varying degrees of optimism about the impact of feminist social work within statutory settings, there has been general agreement about the possibility of women social workers occupying what Dale and Foster have identified as a buffer position: 'Welfare professionals do not invariably oppress female clients. Indeed, in a number of ways the existence of relatively powerful and autonomous welfare professions acts as an important beneficial buffer between women and the patriarchal/capitalist state' (Dale and Foster 1986: 102). From within this position, Hudson has regarded women social workers as possessing a degree of autonomy that can be used to develop more women-sensitive social work policies and practices (Hudson 1985: 654) and both Hallett and Comley have found opportunities for re-negotiating the form and content of services to reflect the needs and capacities of women that can be grasped from within this buffer position (Hallett 1989: x; Comley 1989: 45). The buffer position has been characterised as having a considerable degree of autonomy that women social workers can exploit:

> Social workers, to the extent that the state's objectives are mediated through their practice, occupy an interesting structural position in relation to these dynamics [of struggle] . . . social workers can make effective use of this position . . . [they] need to rethink welfare and the dominant assumptions that mediate its forms and develop strategies that, in practice, can counteract their own involvement in the reproduction of oppressive social relations.
>
> (Comley 1989: 63)

Comley's reference to involvement in the reproduction of oppressive social relations (and see, Comley 1989: 57, 68; Birmingham Women and Social Work Group 1985: 118–120) suggests constraints that women social workers experience within their buffer role in the statutory context. They are, after all, 'firmly located in the state apparatus' (Dominelli 1997: 70). Dominelli has seen this state location as offering little room for professionals to assert their power as professionals (ibid. 72), with social workers being subservient to their paymasters (ibid. 84) and their ability to influence the definition of social work's remit being limited (ibid. 115). She has concluded that: 'The provision of services has become subservient to managerial imperatives, whittling away much of the limited autonomy through which individual professionals have exercised a modicum of control over their own labour process' (Dominelli 1992: 93). Hudson has suggested the need to recognise the limits of what is possible (Hudson, A. 1989: 79) and Brook and Davis have noted hostile reactions from state agencies to women social workers involved in developing feminist forms of social work (Brook and Davis 1985b: xv):

> Social work's espoused primary aim is to promote people's welfare but the way in which this is carried out varies by agency and the legal constraints imposed upon it . . . Statutory work is directly funded by the central and local state and is empowered by law to protect people's personal welfare when that is endangered by themselves or others, and to provide them with the necessary for becoming 'good citizens'. Both these functions are defined in terms that are consistent with prevailing ideology.
>
> (Dominelli and McLeod 1989: 10)

One aspect of the way in which the constraints imposed by prevailing ideology have been identified as being experienced by women social workers is that workers who are engaged in feminist practice are also engaged in other (inegalitarian) work which reinforces various forms of social control over women (Dominelli and McLeod 1989: 125).

What has been struggling to emerge from many of the accounts in the feminist social work literature is that at the core of the statutory context is the authority role (Wise 1985; 1995), played out by social workers in implementing and enforcing duties deriving from statutes, for example, their statutory responsibilities for the care and protection of children. Although Hanmer and Statham have acknowledged that social workers can be placed in the position of working in opposition to women (Hanmer and Statham 1999: 54), conflicts stemming from the authority social workers hold are, for the most part, only hinted at or glimpsed fleetingly in the feminist social work literature, rather than being the subject of sustained discussion.

On the contrary, when feminist social work writers have encountered constraints in integrating their perspectives with social work in statutory settings, there has still been an overriding optimism that this can be achieved: 'Whilst a feminist practice is beset with difficulty and controversy, the problems are not insurmountable and there is scope for feminist social work practice even within a statutory setting' (Hale 1984: 168–169). Similarly, Hudson has suggested that although some of the constraints of working according to feminist principles inside large state-sponsored bureaucracies have been revealed, nevertheless much insight has been gained into the scope for changing social work practice, even within the limitations imposed by existing structures (Hudson, A. 1989: 78–79). There is an overriding belief that, whatever the circumstances, feminist social work, as depicted in the literature, can triumph:

> The institutional parameters of social work provide the means by which the stability of social work practice can be maintained over time. These include organisational, legislative and professional constraints. Constraints do not have to operate in a conservative fashion by controlling 'client' aspirations and demands. Feminist social work has provided an alternative paradigm which has demonstrated that institutions can promote rather than hinder 'client' well-being.
>
> (Dominelli 1997: 137)

This points to constraints being surmounted through changes in the statutory organisation, which is seen as a target of feminist social work intervention.

Transforming the organisational culture of statutory social work has been seen as an essential dimension of feminist practice (Dominelli 1997: 100). Charles has suggested that feminist social movements 'engage with the state by confronting it and by working within it'. The state is experienced by workers 'as both enabling and constraining, as oppressive and responsive to pressure for change' (Charles 2000: 28). Hale has argued that the organisational dimension is a core constituent in seeking to move beyond the pressure to individualise women's experience:

> Without a clear understanding of the patriarchal structure of society, of families and of the organisations in which they work, and an articulated stance

and strategy towards these structures, feminist social workers find it very difficult to survive. If each encounter is perceived as an isolated incident rather than an integral part of a whole system of oppression and if the feminist social worker does not connect with others to examine collectively their common ground, then feelings of frustration, disappointment and isolation are inevitable.

(Hale 1984: 167–168)

Hudson concluded that optimism about the capacity to change employing organisations is one of the fundamental prerequisites for feminist-influenced social work practice (Hudson 1985: 654). Although agreeing with Hudson that feminist social work practitioners should engage with employing organisations, Charles added a note of caution: 'engaging with the state courts the danger that feminist interests will be lost sight of and issues redefined in non-feminist terms'. However, she concurred that 'the state has to be engaged with both internally and externally in order to change its policies and to challenge the gender order' (Charles 2000: 28). Orme has also promoted such an approach: 'Feminist praxis . . . seeks to challenge and transform policy, practice and the organisation of the service delivery, which constrains people in gender-specific roles or oppresses them by the inappropriate exercise of power' (Orme 1998: 227). This broad conception of feminist praxis includes challenging and transforming practice, the final area for consideration in this discussion of feminist social work and the statutory context.

Very few feminist social work writers have drawn directly on examples of practice undertaken by qualified social workers.[2] Dominelli and McLeod (1989) pointed to the existence of feminist practice with service users in statutory social work on a one-to-one and small group basis (Dominelli and McLeod 1989: 114). In the main,[3] they cited as evidence material produced by student social workers whilst on placement (Evans 1985; Warren 1985; Donnelly 1986; Falk 1986). However, it is questionable whether practice on student placements corresponds to that of qualified social workers in terms of work pressure and the amount of interest in, and support for, work with women. Placements could well have involved working with small and protected caseloads under very close supervision (Wise 1985: 5). Thus there has been little evidence of what feminist practice, grounded in the realities of everyday social work, might be like (Wise 1995: 105, 111). An exception is provided by Milner, who has commented on the difficulties she faced when taking time out of an academic post to return to fieldwork practice. Under pressure from a child protection system that scrutinised women, she found herself working with mothers, and ignoring fathers, notwithstanding her commitment to feminist practice (Milner 1993: 48–49; and see 2001). Similarly, Wise has detailed some of the complexities of working with service users in a series of case studies, complexities which would not evaporate if subjected to the practice proposals of the feminist social work literature, and has concluded that she came to believe that feminist social work, defined in terms of working non-oppressively with women, is a fantasy based on a misunderstanding of the nature of local authority social work (Wise 1985: 2).

Conclusion

Women working with women has been regarded by many writers as at the heart of feminist social work. A shared experience of oppression between women social workers and women service users has been seen as the impetus for creating egalitarian relationships. The feminist social work literature has suggested that women social workers can engage in such egalitarian relationships with women service users in seeking the goal of empowerment. The term empowerment has become increasingly popular within social work and has been used in many different ways, one of which is represented by its presence in the feminist social work literature as the goal to be achieved through egalitarian relationships between women social workers and women service users. The use of the term has been the subject of critique on the grounds that the term is not grounded in the realities of practice.

An initial consideration of the statutory context raised questions about the possibilities of realising a feminist identity, expressed in egalitarian relationships with the goal of empowerment. Feminist social work's proposals appeared to face difficulties when placed within the statutory context. With the exception of Wise's work on the realities of practice (1985, 1995) and Langan's critique of empowerment (Langan 1992a, 1998), the statutory context has been insufficiently explored in the literature. This critique has pointed to the importance of exploring the statutory context in more detail. The statutory context lay in the background in the discussion of the feminist social work literature's urging women social workers to align themselves with a feminist social work identity in Chapter 1 and in this chapter's consideration of the literature's advocacy of woman-to-woman egalitarian relationships between service users and social workers with the goal of empowerment. When the statutory context was moved into the foreground, it was noted that the literature has presented feminist social work as a buffer between women service users and the state. This buffer position was discussed, along with some of its constraints, and the literature's limited attention to practice in statutory settings was noted. The discussion raised initial questions concerning the possibilities of realising the aspirations of feminist social work, as depicted in the literature, in a statutory context. That context will be subjected to further scrutiny in Chapter 3.

Chapter 3

State social work

As we saw in Chapters 1 and 2, writers have called upon women social workers to align themselves with and affiliate to a feminist social work identity, as the basis for establishing egalitarian relationships with women service users, with the goal of empowerment. The advocacy of this 'ethic of empowerment' (Wise 1995) has encompassed statutory settings, albeit with some difference of views concerning the relationship between feminist approaches to social work and other theories and methods (see, for example, Langan 1985; Hanmer and Statham 1988; Phillipson 1991; McNay 1992: 48–66).

The assumption underpinning the literature's advocacy of egalitarian relationships and the ethic of empowerment has been that women social workers are able to make choices about the nature of their work with women service users. As a result, the feminist social work literature has focused overwhelmingly on the principles according to which women social workers' practice should proceed in order to achieve their goals and, for the most part, women social workers have been addressed without reference to their position within the statutory context. The literature has provided only occasional glimpses of some of the constraining features that are exerted by that context on the pursuit of egalitarian relationships and the ethic of empowerment. In other words, much of the feminist social work literature has been suspended in a vacuum, isolated from an analysis of the features of the organisational regime of social work that are associated with its location in the state. As such, the proposals in the literature for feminist social work may have contributed to a debate about what women's practice ought to be like, but this is only a partial framework if it is detached from an understanding of the nature of statutory social work as it is. 'The critical characteristics of social work practice ... do not derive from the prescriptions of professional social workers' (Howe 1986: 2); nor, as we will seek to demonstrate, do they necessarily emanate from feminist social work.

For reasons that will become clear as the discussion unfolds, 'state social work' is seen as a term which depicts more accurately the field of social work usually referred to as the 'statutory sector': 'we regard all social work in Britain as coming under state control in some way and therefore being viewed appropriately as state social work' (Dominelli and McLeod 1989: 10). Whilst having some reservations about the use of the term 'state social work' in this all-embracing sense (although it was perhaps prophetic with regard to the state's later colonisation of the voluntary sector, see Harris 2003: Ch. 8), the significance of the state context in designating the nature of social work as far as the 'statutory sector' is concerned is the central theme of this chapter. Accordingly, 'state social work' is the preferred term for what is usually referred to as 'statutory social work'. State social work, it will be argued, shapes the experiences and delimits the practice possibilities of women social workers. The following sections set out the defining features of social work, stressing its location within the state and the statutory duties undertaken by women social workers on behalf of the state.

Social work as a state-mediated profession

An overarching framework within which women social workers' experiences in state social work can be located and classified is provided by Johnson's analysis of professional work (Johnson 1972). Johnson viewed professions as occupational power structures that can be classified into three categories: collegiate, patronage and mediated. In the case of the latter, an agency, usually a state organisation, acts as mediator between the profession and its clientele in deciding the profession's client population and in broad terms what should be provided for the clientele through a legal framework and the overall allocation of resources. By this means, the state acts as the corporate patron of the professionals who provide services on its behalf, through the state's agencies (Johnson 1972: 77). The state delegates power to, and in the process legitimises the status of, the professionals concerned (Hill 1997: 209):

> [These professions] do not resist the extension of state power for they have no choice but to be public employees. On the contrary they generally welcome the extension of state power, for it is the only source of such power as they themselves possess; indeed, these occupational groups owe their very existence to the power of the state.
>
> (Cousins 1987: 97)

Following Johnson, social work can be considered as a state-mediated power structure within and through which women social workers operate: 'Occupational control is not negotiated within social work, or between social work and its clientele, but mediated by the state' (Hugman 1991a: 201). Although Johnson's typology locates and classifies state social work, it does not extend to a consideration of how state mediation shapes the nature of professionals' work. This concern can be addressed through Derber's work (1982, 1983).

Derber's historical approach highlighted the extent to which professionals have become engaged in salaried, rather than independent, employment. He was concerned with the distinctiveness of professional work and, in particular, the manner and extent to which professionals control their work in situations of 'dependent employment', for example dependent state employment (Derber 1983: 309). In order to demonstrate the distinctiveness of professional work, Derber elaborated the way in which such work is controlled. He argued that the potential for control over professional work has, in principle, two components: control over the means of work, that is over the organisation and execution of work, and control over the ends of work, that is over the final product, the goals or purposes of work. He argued that although professionals lack control over the ends to which their work is put, they nevertheless retain considerable autonomy over the means of undertaking their work. Autonomy over the means of undertaking professional work led Derber to suggest that a 'domain of freedom and creativity' exists around 'problems of technique' (Derber 1983: 316), in deciding how the professional's job is carried out.

In the case of social work, its ends are established by the state. It is, in Derber's terms, 'ideologically subordinated', but, he argued, the means by which the state's ends are achieved are in the hands of social workers (and see Hugman 1991a: 202):

> Keeping social workers' focus on individual pathology and away from social oppression was of major importance to state agencies . . . and formed the basis for a highly sophisticated ideological co-option, where social workers' moral concerns for the well-being of their clients could be accommodated in a form of practice which served institutional ends.
>
> (Derber 1983: 333)

Derber's distinction between the ends and means of professional work suggests that women social workers, as state-mediated professionals, may retain considerable degrees of what he termed 'technical autonomy', that is control over the means of carrying out their work (Derber 1983: 335). Mashaw made a similar distinction for some areas of the state (such as social work), proposing what he designated as the 'professional treatment model', which requires the use of specialist skills and intuitive judgements. He argued that in mediating between the state and the service user, professionals are granted discretion to interpret how tasks are performed within general frameworks (Mashaw 1983: Ch. 2), a position supported by Hill: 'The organisational or planning activities at the top of hierarchies set contexts for, but do not necessarily predetermine decision-making at field levels, where very different tasks are performed and very different problems have to be solved' (Hill 1997: 187–188).

The classic study that illustrated the discretion that state-mediated professionals have in deciding upon the means by which they undertake their work was Lipsky's *Street-level Bureaucracy* (1980):

> On the one hand, service is delivered by people to people, invoking a model of human interaction, caring and responsibility. On the other hand, service is delivered through a bureaucracy, invoking a model of detachment and equal

treatment under conditions of resource limitations and constraints, making care and responsibility conditional.

(Lipsky 1980: 71)

Lipsky suggested that in these circumstances street-level bureaucrats have discretion because the nature of the services they provide requires human judgement that cannot be programmed and for which machines cannot substitute (Lipsky 1980: 161). In similar vein Challis has argued that Social Services Departments' implementation of central government legislation requires social workers to have a degree of discretion and autonomy if they are to deal with the idiosyncrasies of people's lives (Challis 1990: 6). Furthermore, Hudson has suggested that it is in the interests of such agencies not to fetter the discretion of street-level bureaucrats because they are engaged in carrying out much of the difficult rationing of services in situations where demand exceeds supply. It is the exercise of the discretion they possess in carrying out this function that is the source of their power over service users (Hudson, B. 1989).

These three concerns – with the difficulty of programming human judgement, the consequent need for the exercise of discretion and the power inherent in its exercise – affect the achievement and retention of state-mediated professional status. The amount and nature of professional discretion (or, in Derber's terms, 'technical autonomy') enjoyed by women social workers, with regard to the means by which they operate within the professional treatment model, is influenced by the impact of three factors on social work in general: 'expertise' – a body of knowledge that can be learned and transmitted; 'indeterminacy' – work within areas of uncertainty which are portrayed as only susceptible to specialist, esoteric and non-transferable professional skills; 'invisibility' – working situations in which detailed surveillance of work is difficult (Hill 1997: 209–210).

Whilst women social workers' claims to the exercise of discretion on the grounds of expertise might be contentious and contested, indeterminacy has been a significant dimension in social work's general claim for a significant degree of discretion in its operations: 'Professional insulation from external controls is likely to be greatest where the outcomes of professional activities are relatively vague and intangible . . . This may be a factor in professional attachment to casework' (Sibeon 1991: 27). Within their casework social workers have been found to exploit indeterminacy in using their own preferred methods of work (Pithouse 1987: 49) and it is the autonomy to do so which has been the basis on which the job is routinely undertaken (Pithouse 1991: 45–46), as an 'invisible trade' (Pithouse 1987).

Women social workers can, then, be regarded as state-mediated professionals, who have a degree of 'technical autonomy' over the means by which they carry out the ends of the state, within a professional treatment model. Moreover, as we saw in Chapter 2, the feminist social work literature has laid claim to the exercise of discretion by women social workers in their work with women service users in stronger terms than the general claims of social work referred to above, namely, on the basis of expertise (feminist social work) and indeterminacy (egalitarian relationships) in the context of invisibility (away from the office). However, the measure of discretion enjoyed by women social workers over the means by which they carry out their work with women service users is employed in relation to the ends of social work; statutory duties undertaken on behalf of the state.

Social work's statutory duties

The legal underpinning of social work, through its mandate of statutory duties, is the tangible manifestation of the state's 'ends' of social work; statutory duties define the responsibilities to be exercised by women social workers on behalf of the state. Anleu has argued that this legal underpinning affects the environment in which social work is practised (Anleu 1992: 41). Howe went beyond seeing the statutory mandate as a contextual consideration that affects social work and, instead, regarded it as determining the nature of social work much more directly (Howe 1986: 160). Aldridge has presented the state as unequivocally shaping social work and setting its agenda in tasks that are determined by the government of the day (Aldridge 1996: 182–183). Social work is, therefore, in a subordinate position both in terms of how it is defined and how it is organised:

> social work is 'overdetermined' by the economic and social formation so that its status is best seen as relatively subordinate rather than as relatively autonomous. Put at its most uncompromisingly straightforward, state welfare is an element within the state apparatus, and as such will be to some extent articulated with it at both ideological and material levels . . . What passes for social work is the product of the varying capacity of certain institutions and agencies to give it particular definition, to shape what it is that constitutes legitimate professional knowledge and the manner in which the delivery of services should be organised. In both respects, this means that the nature of social work is an accomplishment, a construction . . .
>
> (Webb 1996: 173)

It follows that what is considered to be 'social work' is not fixed but will undergo construction and reconstruction as a result of ideological shifts by successive governments, which are reflected in legislative changes (Sheppard 1995: 273). As Jones points out, the tempo may have increased in recent years, but from the late 1940s onwards state social work has not had any sustained period free from significant legislative change (Jones 1999: 38).

As a consequence of the state drawing up the parameters of social work through legislation, women social workers are presented with statutory duties that define certain categories of people who, it has been decided, will be the focus of their work. Thus the core functions of social work are established in the law, as the manifestation of state policy. The law sets out the rights, duties and responsibilities of social work, on the one hand, and of service users, on the other, in those socially problematic areas which have been accorded official recognition by the state. In this way, the law not only defines the ends of social work, but also constitutes the source of women social workers' authority for the means by which they intervene in service users' lives in the exercise of statutory duties. Social work's existence within the state is, therefore, central to the establishment of social workers' right to intervene in aspects of people's lives that are defined as socially problematic (Sheppard 1995: 35). Social work becomes statutory in the act, or more accurately Acts, of the state producing legislation (and accompanying guidelines and procedures), which are directed at certain categories of people, such as the child in need of protection or the older person who needs residential care. Women social workers implement that legislation, in the form of statutory duties, on behalf of the state.

If the delegation of authority to social work, as a mediated profession, is a state strategy dealing with certain social problems in specific and individualised ways, it carries the implication that those social problems to which social work's attention is directed are in the process depoliticised. Parton (1994) has seen this as a contradictory process, namely that the political role of social work is in its being seen as apolitical, as being what he terms elsewhere 'social-work' (Parton 1996a, 1996b). Social problems become personal problems with individual solutions, to be left in the hands of experts (Wilding 1982: 63) working in the personal social services:

> Social workers' concern is not with social problems per se so much as those individuals who are socially defined as socially problematic in areas of concern to the occupation. In this sense, theirs is a case-based approach. The delega-tion of work in these areas of concern reflects the individualising influence of the definitions of the problems themselves . . . When these problems are delegated to social workers, the institutionalised definition of the problems and the appropriate responses constrain the activities of social workers.
>
> (Sheppard 1995: 40)

As Howe succinctly put it, social workers are concerned with 'cases not causes' (Howe 1980: 319). Recognition of this depoliticising effect of the state's delegation of social problems to social work leads Davies to argue that social work can only survive if social workers accept this as the reality of their position and adopt a consensus model, working within existing social relations (Davies 1986).

As a state-mediated profession, social work has, then, been rooted in an overall state policy framework for managing certain areas of social life through the personal social services. The framework is consensus-oriented and individualistic in its determination of the ends of state intervention in social problems. However, we should avoid the temptation to present women social workers' intervention in women service users' lives as a straightforward cause and effect process in which women service users are slotted into particular socially problematic categories, as identified by the state in legislation, and then automatically become service users and the subject of women social workers' attentions. As we saw earlier, the means of achieving the state's ends are delegated to women social workers, as the state's experts in defining who constitutes an individual example of a particular socially problematic category. In the late 1970s and the 1980s, a number of studies demonstrated the significance of social workers' mediating function in the making of key decisions about who became a service user (see, for example, Parsloe and Stevenson 1978; Smith 1980; Buckle 1981; Satyamurti 1981; Kemshall 1986; Pithouse 1987). However, whilst reflecting the pivotal position of social workers as state mediators, these studies did not unpack in any detail the process involved in turning people into service users.

The production of service users through the implementation of statutory duties involves the 'creation of subjects' (Philp 1979). Leonard has argued that traditionally in social work the key to the creation of subjects has been the rhetoric of universalism that has been present in British state policy, carrying within it an assumption of homogeneity (Leonard 1996: 21). Thus, state social work, although targeted at individuals, carefully categorised general needs:

> Under the influence of British social administration, social services . . . were based upon the careful categorisation of client . . . 'needs', supposedly reflecting the generally common needs of integrated coherent subjects rather than the diverse, conflicting and culturally varied needs of different individuals and populations.
>
> (Leonard 1996: 22)

This is the context within which the social worker is involved with the individual subject in the person of the service user and within which the subject position of the service user is constructed (Leonard 1997a). Furthermore, Leonard has argued that although service users may provide a narrative to social workers, and it may be listened to, it is not received as a form of knowledge on a par with the professional knowledge of the expert, which is brought to bear on a service user's individual circumstances. In other words, the service user's narrative is subject to interpretation by professional standards. These are used to make judgements and to bring the service user's narrative into conformity with the state's legal and organisational categories through processes of subjectification and subordination, culminating in the case file (Leonard 1997b: 94–96):

> The clients wait in line and are acted upon 'in their own interests' by the bureaucracy which organises them, their multifarious wants reduced to the manageable entity of a set of defined items requiring attention. To describe the file and its meaning in terms of control and subordination is not to suggest that social service agencies are typically Kafkaesque in their heartless anonymity, though some may be.
>
> (Leonard 1997b: 94)[1]

These transformation processes should not be regarded as a mechanical function. The previous section emphasised that there is room for some variation in forms of practice, that is, the means by which these processes are undertaken. However, these processes cannot occur without the existence, or outside, of the state-defined prescribed roles for social workers in identifying individual examples of socially problematic categories, roles which embody the state's ends, expressed in the statutory duties undertaken. (This becomes clear if we contrast Leonard's quotation above, with the position of independent counsellors who can work, by and large, solely at the level of their clients' individual subjectivity.) Women social workers, in their mediation of the subjectivity of women service users and the state's socially problematic categories, are state agents:

> We can . . . recognise the usefulness of seeing state disciplinary power over . . . its subjects as a gaze, an inspecting, regulating gaze. The history of the welfare state in Western societies might be seen as the refining of this gaze, its technological development, its proliferation through specialisation and professional expertise, its justification as necessary for the subject's well-being . . . 'the gaze' is both a literal description of social practices and a metaphor for the monitoring and surveillance of subjects undertaken by the state apparatus.
>
> (Leonard 1997b: 43)

Conclusion

A dominant stance within the feminist social work literature has regarded women social workers as being able to embrace a feminist identity as the basis for engaging in egalitarian relationships with women service users, which are aimed at the latter's empowerment. In taking this stance, the defining features of social work – as a state-mediated profession charged with implementing statutory duties on behalf of the state – were largely ignored by feminist social work writers. In much of the feminist social work literature, women social workers have been presented as essentially autonomous in making choices about the ends, as well as the means, of their work with women service users, as though the implementation of duties on the state's behalf can be transcended. For example, Dale and Foster, whilst giving a very negative account of how welfare professionals, including social workers, can exercise control over women service users (Dale and Foster 1986: 81), have concluded that:

> One of the key characteristics or skills which professionals are deemed to possess is their ability to define welfare needs. It is because of these special skills that professionals are allowed so much freedom and control over their own services. This basic tenet of professionalism means that professionals will strongly resist any attempts by the state to intervene with or restrict their autonomous definitions of welfare needs.
>
> (Dale and Foster 1986: 103)

In the light of the discussion in this chapter, Dale and Foster's conclusion seems to be a classic example of the conflation of ends and means. Feminist social work writing has tended to conflate ends and means in the same way and, in the process, has implied that social work's statutory context can be transcended. For example, Dominelli has maintained that feminist social workers should be 'seeking compatibility between the ends being sought and the means whereby these are achieved . . . [in] seeking collectivist solutions which respect the individuality and uniqueness of each woman' (Dominelli 1997: 246) and Mullender has suggested that 'gendering the agenda in social work, will improve both the employment context and the commissioning and delivery of every type of service' (Mullender 1997: 48).

The discussion earlier in this chapter would suggest that conflation of ends and means in this fashion, and the consequent assumption of autonomy with which women social workers are deemed to operate, obscures the extent to which working in a state context shapes the ends of the work of women social workers, whilst traditionally having allowed them discretion (or, in Derber's terms, 'technical autonomy'), as state agents, in shaping the means by which those ends are realised. In contrast to the assumption that the statutory context can be transcended, Dominelli and McLeod have argued that 'a feminist theory and practice of social work proceeds from rather different premises than that currently prevailing in statutory social work'. They concluded that if feminist social work is to take root in statutory settings, social work has to be transformed from bases external to statutory social work so that it is more reflective of feminist aims (Dominelli and McLeod 1989: 114). They emphasised the significance of wider political influences:

> It is important to acknowledge the extent of the continued reliance of feminist work in a statutory setting on feminist action external to it . . . It depends on the political complexion of the local and central state governing those agencies . . . Feminist practice within statutory social work can be underwritten and promoted in a major way.
>
> (Dominelli and McLeod 1989: 127)

In contrast to both of these positions (transcending or transforming state social work), Wise, as we saw in Chapter 2, has developed a third position concerning the relationship between feminist social work and state social work, namely that they are antithetical: 'the quest for liberation sits uneasily within the framework of state-provided services . . . [and is] the province of political activists within various social movements' (Wise 1995: 113). On the basis of this distinction, Wise has argued that the term 'feminist social work' should only be retained for alternative services for women that can truly claim to be feminist (Wise 1995: 113). She makes a distinction between feminist social work and anti-discriminatory practice and seeks an accommodation with state social work based on the latter. The analysis of the state context presented in this chapter points in the direction of that context closing off specifically feminist ends for social work and would lend support to the need to question whether there is a case for retaining the term 'feminist social work' with reference to state social work.

In the next chapter, state social work is explored further by examining the organisational regimes of the British welfare state, and more specifically the regimes of Social Services Departments, regimes within which women social workers' experiences are embedded.

Chapter 4

Social work regimes

Chapter 3 established the significance of statutory duties in sanctioning women social workers' intervention in what are identified by the state as those socially problematic areas of women service users' lives that are seen as warranting intervention. Women social workers do not, however, function as atomised individual practitioners, directly connected to the legislation they implement. The statutory mandate of state social work is implemented through organisations. Although women social workers' power and authority is ultimately derived from, and exists to implement, a framework of statutory duties that defines their tasks and functions (Sheppard 1995: 53), they undertake those duties from their employment position within Social Services Departments[1] (Hugman 1991b: 62). This inextricable intertwining of policy, organisation and practice is clearly emphasised in Payne's comment that social work practice can only be understood in the context of policy and organisation, and policy and organisation can only be understood as they are expressed through practice (Payne 1995: xiii). Thus, Social Services Departments are the sites through which central government legislation is mediated through policy and implemented through organisation (Cooper 1991), before being turned by women social workers into concrete practices:

> Social workers emerged from a close relationship with state authority . . . into a typically professional position from which they mediate state power and regulation in indirect ways . . . The internal organisation of the social work profession . . . ensures some minimum of conformity of social workers to the requirements of the state.
>
> (Langan 1985: 43)

Thus, a Social Services Department is not just, as it is often termed, a 'social work agency'; it is the *agency* of social work, the locus within which the state's legislative mandate is carried out in social work roles and tasks (Howe 1979, 1986; Davies 1986).

Social work's bureau-professional regime

The general historical appeal of state bureaucracies, such as Social Services Departments, can be readily understood, as they were regarded as an advance on earlier organisational regimes in their being structures based upon equality before the law and notions of order, reason and justice (Leonard 1997b: 89). The specific appeal of state bureaucracy for social work, which led eventually to the establishment of Social Services Departments, can be traced back to the foundation of the post-war welfare state. It was an appeal in which organisation and professionalism were 'inescapably linked' (Hugman 1991a: 200).

In the aftermath of World War II there was some debate about whether social work had a role to play in the newly established social democratic welfare state (Seed 1973: 49–52). The resolution of this debate lay in state social work being seen as humanising and fine-tuning citizens' contact with the welfare state:

> The social worker who does for the run of ordinary people what confidential secretaries and assistants do for the favoured few is putting a genuine professional skill at the disposal of those who may properly be called her clients and she is as essential to the functioning of a welfare state as is lubrication to the running of an engine. Without her the machinery would seize up.
>
> (Wootton 1959: 298–299)

This representation of social work, as the individualising and personalising arm of the welfare state, masked social work's state-derived power and authority, discussed in the previous chapter. However, the notion of the social worker as a state-provided confidential secretary resonated with the dominant social democratic ideology. From within that ideology, Marshall's view was that the state was no longer concerned with providing for the 'helpless and hopeless' of the population but had shifted to focusing on the welfare of all citizens. He identified an emergent consensus, with increasing agreement on the services that the state should provide and support for the idea of the overall responsibility for the welfare of the citizen remaining with the state (Marshall 1965: 97). From within this consensus, Marshall (1981: 141–142) viewed service users as clients who submitted themselves to the ministrations of the benign state (Roche 1987: 369), passively consuming provision provided by professionals (Keane 1988: 4). The assumption of client passivity in the face of professional expertise was built into the organisational regime that was constructed for the delivery of social services (Marshall 1975: 205–206), namely 'bureau-professionalism'.

Bureau-professional regimes combined two dimensions in the organisation of state welfare provision: the rational administration of bureaucratic systems and professional expertise, and discretion in control over the content of services (Clarke and Langan 1993: 67). Bureau-professionalism was rooted in Fabian assumptions about the correct combination of professional expertise and the regulatory principles of rational administration as the route to social welfare (Newman and

Clarke 1994: 22). Clarke and Newman have regarded this combination as containing two modes of co-ordination: 'bureaucratic co-ordination' – efficient and impartial administration; 'professional co-ordination' – expertise that involved more than administrative competence and drew on distinctive bodies of knowledge and skills about the causes of, and solutions to, social problems (Clarke and Newman 1997: 5–6).

These professional and bureaucratic modes of co-ordination were, however, 'always constrained by the political will of representative democracy' (Leonard 1997b: 101), through which different social interests were mediated:

> Between the late 1940s and the mid-1970s, it is possible to see the welfare state as being sustained by a triple social neutrality: first, the bi-partisan political settlement . . . ; second, bureaucratic administration which promised social impartiality; and third, professionalism which promised the application of valued knowledge in the service of the public . . . These three principles – of political representation, bureaucratic administration and professionalism – combined in different ways and with different balances of power in specific institutional arrangements.
>
> (Clarke and Newman 1997: 8)

Bureau-professional regimes thus combined bureaucratic, professional and political modes of power linking policy-making (politics), policy implementation (bureaucracy) and practice (professionalism) (Newman and Clarke 1994: 23). Clarke and Newman have identified three particular power formations in traditional bureau-professional regimes: 'decision-making power' – the application of bureaucratic rules to particular cases and the exercise of professional discretion involving the application of specialised knowledge to complex cases or processes; 'agenda-setting power' – the capacity to define what decisions need to be made, centred on connecting formalised categories of need to the assessment of individual cases (i.e. the identification and assessment of need and the application of expertise to meeting legitimated needs); 'normative power' – the bureau-professional discourse of needs and rights, through which access to services must be negotiated, legitimating professional expertise and discretion (Clarke and Newman 1997: 63).

Bureau-professionalism was, then, a specific configuration of structures, cultures, relationships and processes of organisational co-ordination whose detailed manifestations varied according to specific contexts (Newman and Clarke 1994: 22–23). In the case of state social work, a key manifestation was the implementation of the Seebohm Report in local authorities. As a consequence of the implementation of the report, social work became a more central element of the welfare state (Clarke 1979: 127). Social work's position, as a state-mediated profession (see Chapter 3), was thus consolidated through the establishment of a bureau-professional organisational regime. In the implementation of the Seebohm Report, both bureaucratic managerial structures and professionalism were combined:

> In 1970 the new Social Services Departments came into being . . . involving
> . . . a blending of elements of professionalism and bureaucratic organisation.
> Neither autonomous professionalism nor purely bureaucratic hierarchies
> emerged from the reorganisation . . . This mode of organisation . . . is a hybrid,
> which we shall refer to as bureau-professionalism . . . It involved a negotiated
> partnership between social work, attempting to organise as a profession on
> the one hand, and the managerial and organisational approach of the state and
> local authorities on the other.
>
> (Parry and Parry 1979: 42–43)

Within this bureau-professional organisational regime, a bureaucratic hierarchy
was compatible with the employment of professional discretion by social workers
(Webb and Wistow 1987: 107–108) or, in Derber's terms, 'technical autonomy'
over the means of carrying out their work (see Chapter 3). This regime provided
women social workers with the organisational base for the power they exercised
in their work with women service users and their organisational position within
bureau-professionalism gave them their day-to-day authority. Bureau-professional
regimes were imbued from the outset with a strong streak of authoritarianism
(Roche 1992: 37), with little concern for professionals' accountability to service
users (Johnson 1972; Wilding 1982; Hugman 1991b). This authority dimension
was disguised by the dominant social democratic ideology, but was nevertheless
present:

> Bureau-professional relationships were characterised by the power of such
> staff to categorise, define and treat service users. That is, they were able
> to deploy decision making, agenda setting and normative power within the
> scope of individual client/worker interactions . . . In bureau-professional
> interactions, the power of service users was based on limited entitlements
> to certain universal services . . . They had little power to influence the ways
> in which services were delivered or the processes through which bureau-
> professional power was enacted.
>
> (Clarke and Newman 1997: 63–64)

Critiques of this authoritarian aspect of bureau-professionalism, as a linchpin
of the post-war welfare state, became crucial to how women social workers fared
with the emergence of new managerialism.

Social work and managerialism

As we have seen, state social work was characterised by three features in the
post-war welfare state, and more especially in the post-Seebohm era: it was a state-
mediated occupation, it was charged with the exercise of statutory duties and
it was located within a bureau-professional regime. Social work has remained a
state-mediated occupation charged with the exercise of statutory duties but its

organisational regime has changed fundamentally. This fundamental shift was achieved by managerialism, 'the term used to refer to the inroads made by management into professional autonomy and power' (Clarke *et al*. 1994: 6–7). Social work was ripe for incursion by managerialism as a result of being identified by the Thatcher governments as one example of the social democratic welfare state's legacy in the organisational, professional and political power of bureau-professional regimes, a legacy identified as an obstacle to the reform of the welfare state in the 1980s (Clarke *et al*. 1994: 3; Clarke and Newman 1993: 48–49; Newman and Clarke 1994: 23).

From the 1980s onwards, an emphasis on managerialism as a transformational force occupied an increasingly significant role in the organisation of state welfare regimes (Pollitt 1990; Clarke *et al*. 1994). Managerialisation was a strategy for the recomposition and diminution of the previous modes of power within the welfare state in order to establish the conditions for enhanced managerial control (Newman and Clarke 1994: 25). During the Thatcher governments, recasting social democratic structures and cultures through managerialism (Clarke *et al*. 1994: 4), using management models derived from the private sector, was seen as the key to reconstituting the public sector and harmonising public and private regimes through the introduction of the three Es – effectiveness, efficiency and economy (Local Government Training Board 1985; Audit Commission 1988; Pollitt 1990: 27; Hoggett 1991):

> The managerialism current in public service organisations . . . has sought to install effectiveness, efficiency and economy as the overriding principles of sound management . . . By redefining clients as consumers and emphasising the virtues of 'choice' and 'diversity', it has attempted to infuse welfare practice with something resembling market discipline. Aided by the work of the Audit Commission it has defined or rather redefined accountability in largely financial terms. The result is supposedly the leaner and meaner organisation geared to flexible response on a fast-changing welfare terrain . . . Welfare must be seen to be done rather than said to be done. Recognisable results and the primacy of the product over process are what matters in managerialised organisations.
>
> (Froggett and Sapey 1996: 9)

After the 1987 general election, state social work began to experience managerialism to a greater extent than previously, with the passing of legislation aimed at controlling expenditure, dividing up public provision, increasing the scope of the private sector, strengthening business management principles and reducing the influence of professionals (Jones 1994: 190, 205). This was depicted as a 'revolutionary' process by the Audit Commission (Audit Commission 1988: 1) that required social work to be more managerial in a changing legislative context, shaped by the Children Act 1989 and the National Health Service and Community Care Act 1990.

These twin pillars of social work's legislative mandate originated in different policy-making processes and displayed differences in policy goals (Hallett 1991) but government guidance sought to emphasise similarities in their approach (Department of Health 1989: para. 1.3; 1990: para. 1.18). Langan concluded:

> Although Social Services Departments and social workers survived, and were in a sense legitimated by the welfare legislation of the late eighties, they emerged in the 1990s with new roles and with circumscribed powers and prestige. The framework for both community care and child protection increased central government control and extended multi-agency collaboration on terms which inevitably reduced the authority of Social Services Departments and the autonomy of social workers. The intrusion of surrogate or 'quasi'-markets and the new managerialism on the one hand, and the law and the courts on the other, impose limitations on social workers' professional aspirations.
>
> (Langan 1993: 149–150)

Elsewhere Langan pointed specifically to implications for women in the legislation through the ideological focus on traditional family values in the Children Act 1989 and the promotion of extended kinship networks in the NHS and Community Care Act 1990 (Langan 1992b: 84).

As part of this process of legislative reform, Preston-Shoot detected a shift away from the law being seen as representing the ends of the state (see Chapter 3) – ends to which the means of social work practice were directed – and towards the law becoming the definition of practice itself, thus implying a diminution in social workers' role in mediating the implementation of the law. 'Legalism' has been regarded as replacing practice based on other conceptions of social work and as marginalising social work's mediating role in representing service users' experiences to their employing organisations (Preston-Shoot 1996: 49; and see Braye and Preston-Shoot 1998: 60–61). The increasing trend towards legalism has been regarded as having been transmitted into practice via agency policies and priorities and, in the process, social work's knowledge base, values and core activities were said to have been lost (Preston-Shoot 1996: 52). It has been argued that government guidance and local management began to prescribe in detail the legally based criteria for decisions and that this left little scope for individual judgement and skill (Jones and Jordan 1996: 257).

The increasing influence of managerialism under Conservative governments during the 1990s, in defining agency policies and priorities in social work, as elsewhere in the public sector, resulted in the development of three interlocking strategies of control: decentralising operational units concurrent with achieving a greater degree of centralised control over strategy and policy; establishing the principle of managed competition; and developing processes of performance management and monitoring (audits, inspections, quality assessments, reviews), largely directed towards operationally decentralised units (Hoggett 1996). In relation to social work, the implementation of the NHS and Community Care Act 1990 involved the development of all three control strategies simultaneously. The implementation of the Children Act 1989 witnessed a minimal amount of managed competition but the other two control strategies have been used (Packman and Jordan 1991; Otway 1996; Parton 1996b). Hoggett (1996), and others, have identified a number of effects that stemmed from these three managerial control strategies. First, decentralised units became more like small businesses, making it difficult to transcend the particularity of the experience of working in a specific unit. Second, central government's hold was strengthened. The arrival of managerialism was accompanied and promoted by detailed policy and practice guidance, encapsulated in procedures, as an alternative to the exercise of professional discretion (Froggett and Sapey 1996: 11). There was:

> A massive growth in detailed sets of guidance, procedures and checklists. In addition to government guidance, each agency is developing its own codes of practice and procedures . . . this proceduralization can be viewed as a way of circumscribing professional autonomy and discretion.
>
> (Banks 1998: 214)

As a result, practitioners became more likely to be concerned with the measurable outcomes of depoliticised practice (see Chapter 3), as they followed departmental and government rules, guidance and procedural manuals (Everitt 1998: 109). This enabled them to be depicted as 'passive agents of management systems' (Huntington 1999: 244), whose 'professional autonomy has been circumscribed and practice increasingly standardised' (Huntington 1999: 242). For entrants to social work, such organisational compliance has been seen as an increasingly valued and crucial quality (Harlow 2003: 37), as Jones has emphasised:

> In the contemporary welfare system, state social work agencies do not require highly informed or educated, research-aware social workers. These are now regarded as positively unhelpful qualities that make for questioning and criticism. Rather what is now demanded is agency loyalty, an ability to follow instructions, to complete procedures and assessments on time, to modify and placate client demand, to manage inadequate budgets and to work in such ways that will not expose the agency to public ridicule.
>
> (Jones quoted in Harris, 2003: 113)

Third, whilst control over resources was delegated increasingly to operational managers, centralised control was retained and strengthened over key strategic questions such as the allocation of resources to operational units, within a framework of financial rules and performance targets (Hoggett 1991). This meant that social workers had to learn cost-consciousness:

> In a short space of time the British personal social services were transformed from agencies with . . . considerable professional autonomy and discretion,

into systems that deploy expert knowledge to manage risks and needs in ways
that are highly responsive to price signals.

(Jones and Jordan 1996: 257)

Fourth, distributive questions were depoliticised as the overall volume of
demand which was allowed to be met was fixed by cash limits allocated to cost
centres. In times of budgetary constraint, operational decentralisation combined
with tightly centralised expenditure control restrains costs, as budget-holders strive
to stay within budget (Payne 1995: 79). This is often referred to, somewhat cos-
metically, as concentrating on 'core business'; shedding activities that do not
contribute to the organisation's primary goals, with the interplay between external
or statutory requirements and internal organisational politics constructing specific definitions of core business in particular organisations (Clarke and Newman
1997: 78). In the process, difficult rationing decisions, stemming from how
'core business' or 'core services' are defined, are passed down the line to social
workers.

Fifth, surveillance increased. Traditional supervision was increasingly supplemented or replaced by invisible surveillance by computer and this was accompanied
by greater formalisation through form-filling, report writing and procedure
following (Newman and Clarke 1994: 20; Leonard 1997b: 91; Harris 2003:
Ch. 4). Invisible surveillance was complemented by visible surveillance through
audit and evaluation of explicit and measurable organisational objectives (Clarke
and Newman 1997: 118) by bodies such as the Social Services Inspectorate,
the Audit Commission (Kelly 1992; Jones and Novak 1994), Joint Reviews
(Humphrey 2002, 2003a, 2003b) and, more recently, the Commission for Social
Care Inspection. This has led to social work organisations focusing on impression
management and performing to target (Clarke and Newman 1997: 80–81; Harris
2003: Ch. 5).

Although managerialism was ushered in by Conservative governments, and
the five effects reviewed above had emerged before New Labour took power in
1997, with New Labour's arrival managerialism was reinvigorated and consolidated (Hall 1998). New Labour's social policy has owed much to the neo-liberal
legacy of the Conservative governments (Lister 2000; Butler and Drakeford 2001a,
2001b): 'The election of New Labour in 1997 [did] not herald any kind of decisive
break – at least as far as state social work and its clients [were] concerned – in the
neo-liberal project' (Jones 2001: 550).

This continuation of the neo-liberal political project has been depicted as a
process of 'Third Way' modernisation (Blair 1998); a process regarded as essential
if public sector services were to be brought into line with what are seen as the
superior practices of the private sector in order to achieve continuous improvements
in both quality and cost through the search for 'best value' (Department of the
Environment, Transport and the Regions 1998). More specifically in relation to
social work, the *Modernising Social Services* White Paper (Department of Health
1998) and the *Quality Strategy for Social Care* (Department of Health 2000)

stressed the importance of local performance measures against which progress within an agreed timescale could be monitored in support of implementation of best value (ibid. para. 31).

Underpinning this process of Third Way modernisation is an emphasis on choice:

> The idea that public services should enable individuals and households to choose between alternative suppliers of health, education and social care makes sense only within a particular version of how such decisions construct a just and viable social order. This model argues that social institutions, such as families, communities and markets, merge and adapt because they deliver the most reliable sources of well-being for human populations; and that the best way to create sustainable social systems is to give such individuals and households scope for these decisions and for moving about, under the momentum of their own desires and preferences, within these institutions.
>
> (Jordan 2005: 429–430)

Individual choice has been promoted as desirable and seen as the main force for change in transforming citizens from passive recipients of the state's help into 'active self-sustaining individuals' (Clarke 2005: 448–449), with collectivism rejected in favour of autonomy, rooted in choice and commodified service packages (Jordan 2005: 433).

Some writers have considered that there has been a lack of clarity about where New Labour places social work in this modernised welfare regime (see, for example, Orme 2001). In contrast, other writers (see, for example, Jordan and Jordan 2000; Butler and Drakeford 2001a) have argued that social work has become an aspect of an incorporative agenda, predominantly geared to ensuring that troublesome individuals are made to accept prevailing social norms, rather than seeking inclusiveness in a way that permits more progressive forms of practice, with Butler and Drakeford, for example, lamenting the removal of social work's 'radicalism and transformatory potential' (ibid. 7).

The overall implications of these developments, from the Conservative governments' promotion of managerialism through to New Labour's modernisation agenda, do not augur well for feminist social work. The overall concerns are with economy, efficiency and effectiveness, narrowly defined, with value for money in the production of services. Individual results are measured by outputs that are technically measured and managerially controlled, in contrast to valuing the social/collective outcomes of social work. The assumption is that all service users and situations can be individually classified from within a manageable number of categories, from which service criteria can be developed and linked to delivery of specific outputs. The cost of services can be specified and the efficiency of services measured. Contrary to the feminist social work literature's stance, managerialism is not concerned with the details of women service users' lives or the complexity of factors that may be causing their problems. In order to make problems manageable, the technical efficiency of social workers is the yardstick.

It is tempting to regard these sweeping changes as representing the decisive victory of managerialism and the ousting of bureau-professionalism. However, Clarke and Newman (Clarke and Newman 1997: 76; and see Newman and Clarke 1994: 25) have suggested that new managerialism re-adjusted, rather than displaced, bureau-professionalism. They have identified two main ways in which the relationship between bureau-professionalism and new managerialism has been shaped. The first is through the subordination of bureau-professionalism to new managerialism, requiring professionals to take into account the reality and responsibility of budgetary management so that professional assessments of need take place alongside calculations of the resourcing of intervention. Subordination is a way of containing

> the 'irresponsible' exercise of professional judgement about needs by making it coterminous with the allocation of resources. Where 'need' was once the product of the intersection of bureaucratic categorisation and professional judgement, it is now increasingly articulated with and disciplined by a managerial calculus of resources and priorities.
>
> (Clarke and Newman 1997: 76)

The second way in which Clarke and Newman have identified the relationship between managerialism and bureau-professionalism as having been re-shaped is through co-option, as managerialism has colonised professional concerns and language, bringing them into line with those of management. One example of co-option has been the increasing managerial emphasis on the quality of services rather than simply a calculative view of their efficiency. This managerial attention to service matters builds professionals' attachment to corporate cultures and directions (Clarke and Newman 1997: 76). However, both subordination and co-option require practitioners and managers to demonstrate conformity to organisational policies and procedures (Braye and Preston-Shoot 1998: 58), with a low tolerance level for deviation from conformity in corporate cultures that stand for homogeneity and predictability (Itzin and Newman 1995: 107).

Empirical research into the impact of the changes that have been discussed reveals a mixed response from social workers. In a study conducted by La Valle and Lyons, social workers felt that the more satisfying aspects of the job were being neglected. These neglected aspects were identified as direct work with service users including support and counselling. They also saw the imposition of standards and procedures as an attack on professional autonomy and discretion. However, they approved of the consolidation and formalisation of principles for practice as clarifying the role of the social worker and addressing the power imbalance between professionals and service users (La Valle and Lyons 1996a; 1996b). Similarly, Ellis *et al.* found that social workers viewed formalisation of assessment as a threat to good practice but identified strongly with its objectives of consistency of approach and service user involvement (Ellis *et al.* 1999). In relation to the latter, Irving and Gertig's study of social workers' perceptions of care management indicated their general approval, with social workers welcoming 'the clarity and formalisation of good practice that care management had brought' (Irving and Gertig 1998: 6). More critical voices emerged from a later study by Jones, which revealed that 'social workers felt they were no longer trusted or acknowledged for their skills and abilities' (Jones 2001: 552). These practitioners reported a new working environment within state social work, 'a new type of highly regulated and much more mundane and routinised relationship with clients which could not be described as social work, at least not in the terms that they understood it' (ibid. 552). Similarly, Postle found social workers in her study who were 'demoralised/disillusioned/confused' and 'a small number of staff who coped with the work in a way which no longer involved questioning its inherent dissonances' through a client-processing mentality (Postle 2001: 20; and see Postle 2002).

The implications of organisational restructuring for the framing of face-to-face contact between social workers and service users have been subjected to detailed analysis by Howe. He has argued that the neo-liberal project has altered what 'social work practice' means (Howe 1996: 93). He has also identified the dominant trends as the proceduralisation and commodification of social work (Howe 1994) but has elaborated some of the processes involved (Howe 1996).

First, service users' behaviour is no longer analysed in an attempt to explain it. The service user's performance matters, not what caused it to come about. Behaviour is assessed in terms of administrative procedures, political expectations and legal obligations:

> Depth explanations based on psychological and sociological theories are superseded by surface considerations. It is the visible surface of social behaviour which concerns practitioners and not the internal workings of psychological and sociological entities . . . Clients arrive, in effect, without a history; their past is no longer of interest. It is their present and future performance which matters. Present behaviour, which under a welfare perspective was understood with reference to past experiences, is now assessed in terms of future expectations . . . The evolution and development of individual personalities and social structures is downplayed.
>
> (Howe 1996: 88–89)

Second, as a consequence, there is a breakdown of causal narratives and service users' accounts of their problems are not located and understood within a theoretical perspective whose principles govern what is said and done (Howe 1996: 90). Third, in the absence of narrative, understanding and planned action are re-formed in the immediate context, where the service user's behaviour, needs and responses meet the social worker's rules, resources and procedures and out of such meetings arise agreements, tasks and time limits (Howe 1996: 90). Leonard describes this process as leading to 'each episode of social work intervention [as] discrete and unrelated to the previous episode. Work is short-term, time-limited and brief. Each new encounter triggers a fresh set of transactions, negotiations and agreements' (Leonard 1997b: 90–91).

Finally, intervention involves classification of the service user and a matching response:

> Social workers . . . identify and classify them as particular types of service user or problem-presenters. Having identified and classified the client, he or she is then eligible to receive a certain, prescribed response. This response may be a particular service, a required legal procedure or a certain kind of resource . . . There is no requirement to explore the causes of behaviours and situations, only the demand that they be described, identified and classi-fied. It is the category into which the client's behaviour or condition fits which increasingly determines the response prescribed. The social worker is not encouraged to have independent thoughts but is required to act competently. The emphasis is on what people do rather than what people think.
>
> (Howe 1996: 91)

Clearly the implications of Howe's analysis of developments in practice are significant for the central claims of the feminist social work literature in rela-tion to feminist identity, egalitarian relationships and empowerment. If 'depth explanations' are out of vogue, if present performance is all that matters and if 'causal narratives' have broken down, then the central precepts of the feminist social work literature, along with any other perspectives seeking to move below the surface of the problems presented to state social work, will experience greater difficulty in articulating its concerns and interests in the changed organisational regime.

Youll has adopted a more optimistic stance than Howe's in relation to the nature of practice introduced by new managerialism. She saw new managerialism's emphasis on outputs and outcomes, as represented in central government guide-lines, as a welcome departure from a preoccupation with process because in focusing on ends it moved away from over-rigid prescriptions and towards more creative and flexible approaches to practice (Youll 1996: 36). Dominelli has taken a similar position:

> The British government is using social policy and legislative instruments to restructure the context within which social work has to operate. The Children Act, 1989, the National Health Service and Community Care Act, 1990 . . . have fundamentally altered the statutory environment within which prac-titioners operate. In giving more choice to consumers and casting these in terms of citizens' rights, these developments have provided a supportive backdrop for anti-oppressive practice.
>
> (Dominelli 1998b: 12)

However, as we saw earlier, the realignment of bureau-professionalism with managerial regimes and the latter's emphasis on choice did not necessarily displace bureau-professionalism. Needs are still the subject of 'expert transformation' through the process of assessment (Clarke and Newman 1997: 115), but organisational realignment has led to managerialism infiltrating bureau-professionalism's three modes of power – decision-making, agenda-setting and normative, discussed earlier (Clarke and Newman 1997: 82). However, Clarke and Newman have argued that the ways in which managerialism is interpreted, adapted and resisted by groups and individuals cannot be simply read off from its existence (Clarke and Newman 1997: 82). Managerialisation involves struggles over meaning, involving

> the inflection of new patterns in pursuit of diverse occupational, organisational and social purposes. From this standpoint, managerialism is itself a field of possibilities, open to local processes of resistance, appropriation and compromise. But it also constitutes a field of normative and discursive constraints. It is the dominant formation in the field of contending positions that shape institutionalised outcomes. It forms the terrain that other positions have to negotiate, accommodate to or inflect with in practice . . . Managerialism has set the 'rules of engagement' – the field of constraints – without having the capacity to determine the outcomes.
>
> (Clarke and Newman 1997: 105)

Having explored some of the implications of managerial developments for the organisational restructuring of social work and the impact of developments on practice, we now turn to their impact on women in management.

Social work and women in management

Bureau-professional regimes, prior to the introduction of new managerialism, were depicted as predominantly masculine (Witz 1992). Otway has argued that this gendering of social work hierarchies continued into the era of new managerialism: '[It] is inherent in the framing and execution of the new guidelines and policies and has come about by a masculinisation of the managerial role and hierarchy within Social Services Departments' (Otway 1996: 153). The masculinisation of management is one of the most consistent themes in the feminist social work literature (Hale 1984: 167, 181–182; Davis and Brook 1985: 4; Hudson 1985: 641; Hanmer and Statham 1988: 99–100; Eley 1989; Hallett 1989: Ch.1; Hudson 1989: 86; Butler and Wintram 1991: 23; Dominelli 1991: 184, 190–192; Day 1992: 25–26; Lupton 1992; Hudson et al. 1994: 101–103; Hallett 1996: 12; Davis 1996: 122–125; Dominelli 1997: 250; 2002b: 125; Mullender 1997: 42; Orme 1998: 218; Foster 2004; McPhail 2004), with the emphasis on the way in which 'social work as a profession reproduces the common patriarchal pattern of women making up the base of the pyramid of management with men occupying the summit' (Dominelli and McLeod 1989: 113).

Reflecting on the bureau-professional regime introduced following the Seebohm Report (1968), Hudson concluded that:

> Social work's organisational structures have been highly influential in keeping feminism at bay . . . Post-Seebohm social work organisations have increasingly been structured around managerial principles. The means and methods for delineating social work priorities have become more and more based upon hierarchical principles of decision-making . . . In reality the structure and control of social work reflects and reinforces broader social processes of male domination in our society. Feminism's central emphasis on women participating in the decisions affecting them (as consumers and as workers) and on creating decision-making structures which are non-hierarchical very directly confronts the masculine organisational principles of social work agencies.
>
> (Hudson 1985: 640–641)

In a consideration of the impact of new managerialism, Lupton identified the continuation of this trend in

> An increased marginality for feminist thought and practice within social services departments. The more extensive the masculinisation of the departments' organisational cultures under the impact of the new managerialism, the more overtly masculinised will be the knowledge systems generated . . . It is likely that feminist-inspired research will be seen to deliver the wrong kind of knowledge, collected in the wrong kind of way, about the wrong kinds of things.
>
> (Lupton 1992: 102)

This perception of continuity in, and the intensification of, masculine organisational culture from bureau-professionalism through to new managerialism has been questioned, with new managerialism having been seen as possibly offering new opportunities for women (Newman 1994: 182). Clarke and Newman have identified some of the tensions and discontinuities initiated by new managerialism, which they have seen as having eroded the masculine nature of previous bureau-professional regimes (Clarke and Newman 1997: 69–75). First, 'management' is no longer a term which applies only to the most senior levels. As managerial positions have been created lower down in hierarchies, more women have been drawn into jobs with managerial titles and responsibilities. Second, some women have entered the higher (male) managerial preserves, albeit in highly gendered regimes of managerial power. Third, the gender dynamics of new managerialism are contradictory. The emphasis on leaner and fitter organisations has led to increased macho-management but the people orientation of new managerialism, which is a more relational approach, has led to a partial feminisation of management with a stress on communication skills, networks and partnerships. Fourth, the intensification of emotional labour with service users and within organisations has similarly stressed the importance of 'feminine' management qualities, as management focuses on containment of uncertainty, stress and discontent.

Walton has concluded that the new managerialism is made for men and that women continue to be discriminated against in terms of access to the most senior management posts. He sees women as having realised the possibilities envisaged by Clarke and Newman in the advances they have made at other levels of management but he has questioned whether these advances have had any significant impact:

> My personal impression is that women have made advances in the second, third and fourth tiers of social services management and are making their mark. But it remains an enigma that whereas individual female social workers often have an awareness of women's oppression in their work with individuals and families, social services management staff, whether male or female, do not systematically examine the oppressed position of women.
>
> (Walton 2005: 599)

Conclusion

This chapter has explored the significance of organisational regimes as the locus for attempts to develop feminist social work and has identified the shift from bureau-professional to new managerialist regimes in the provision of state social work. It was noted that bureau-professional regimes located professional discretion within a bureaucratic hierarchy in a way that was conducive to women social workers enjoying a considerable degree of autonomy in their work with women service users. With the arrival of managerialism under the Conservative governments and its reinvigoration under New Labour's 'Third Way' modernisation, individual choice has been emphasised and collectivism has been rejected. Social work has become incorporated into this modernisation agenda, predominantly in terms of having a role in ensuring that troublesome individuals accept prevailing social norms, rather than through seeking more progressive forms of practice. These developments seem to run counter to the development of the forms of practice advocated in the feminist social work literature. In this context, the implications of the changes in social work's organisational regimes for women's prospects in management and their potential to bring about change from the occupation of management positions have received a mixed response.

The next chapter considers the extent and manner in which women's perspectives have been incorporated in the changing patterns of social work education and training that have focused on the reconstitution of what is seen as legitimate professional knowledge and the reconstruction of educational structures. This will be the final thread in contextualising the experiences of women social workers.

Chapter 5

Social work education

Chapters 3 and 4 have set out the defining characteristics of state social work and reviewed the changes in its organisational regime, from the bureau-professionalism which followed the implementation of the Seebohm Report, through to the impact of managerialism. In parallel with the implementation of the Seebohm Report, social work education was brought within a professional validation framework through the establishment of the Central Council for the Education and Training of Social Workers (CCETSW) in 1971.

For much of the 1970s and 1980s, this professional validation framework was permissive by today's standards, with social work education enjoying an academic variant of 'professional self-regulation' (Jones 1999: 37). It was in this context that feminist social work emerged (see Chapters 1 and 2), with social work education providing the main location for its articulation. However, in the 1980s and 1990s CCETSW instituted a process of reform in social work education, which culminated in the restructuring of the arrangements for providing social work programmes and the reshaping of their content. As a result of the reform process, a significant measure of academic self-regulation was replaced by external regulation. This assertion of state authority over social work education reinforced, and served as another avenue for, the tendency of managerialism to encroach on women social workers' practice. With the advent of New Labour, state authority over social work courses was consolidated. CCETSW was abolished and its functions were replaced by the Training Organisation for the Personal Social Services (TOPSS), charged with developing national occupational standards, and the General Social Care Council (GSCC), accorded the responsibility of validating university courses developed in accordance with those standards.

This chapter analyses the changes that have taken place in social work education and its organisational arrangements as a further contributory factor in the shaping of women social workers' practice. An historical overview charts the developments in social work education, drawing on CCETSW, GSCC and other documents, as well as literature commenting on them. The next section considers how 'feminist concerns' were incorporated in the reformulation of social work education by CCETSW and two further sections then draw out the dimensions of competence and partnership as key aspects of that reformulation. New Labour's modernisation of the social care workforce is seen as the context in which subsequent reforms to social work education were located.

Historical overview

1970s: debate and indecision

Having been established by central government in 1971, CCETSW set in place the Certificate of Qualification in Social Work, as the recognised professional qualification that it validated. During the late 1970s, CCETSW was engaged in a wide-ranging consultation process with educational institutions, social work agencies and professional bodies about the future direction of higher education social work programmes. CCETSW published three consultative documents. The third of these documents, written by an assistant director of CCETSW, attracted the most attention (CCETSW 1977). At the time, it was widely regarded as a controversial intervention in the debate about the future of social work education and sparked intense coverage in the social work press. It would appear that CCETSW had anticipated the furore that followed its publication, given the care with which the organisation distanced itself from the document, neither formally endorsing it nor even putting it to CCETSW's Council for discussion. CCETSW's Council did, however, agree to its circulation (CCETSW 1977: 1).

In today's terms, *Consultative Document 3*'s central proposal, which sparked such controversy at the time, was modest in scope; namely, the suggestion that senior staff at CCETSW should seek to arrive at a statement about the aims of the then professional qualification – the Certificate of Qualification in Social Work (CQSW) – and the type of social workers that the programmes validated to provide the CQSW were aiming to produce. The document identified considerable variation in the approaches taken by social work programmes. This was seen as positive but as needing to be supplemented by more emphasis on shared outcomes. In a foreword to the document, Priscilla Young, Director of CCETSW, stated: 'Although diversity is desirable in the style and detail of qualifying courses, a more clearly defined and explicit identity of purpose is needed' (CCETSW 1977: 2).

From the range of issues raised in *Consultative Document 3*, one of the most significant was the proposal that social work programmes should instil in student social workers a 'system of shared professional values, to enable them to begin to practise competently' (CCETSW 1977: 10). This proposal was widely interpreted as an attack on 'progressive' or 'radical' approaches to social work, such as feminist social work, especially as the document went on to advocate that students should seek 'a balance between individualist and collectivist interests' (CCETSW 1977: 12), eschewing action to 'change the system' (CCETSW 1977: 11), as social workers were 'agents of controlled social change' (CCETSW 1977: 11). However, despite such (for that time) forcefully worded statements about CQSW programmes, CCETSW's official position was that 'it is not consistent with the Council's general approach to education and training for social work to establish national requirements for a uniform curriculum' (CCETSW 1977: 6).

Social work programmes were highly critical in their response to *Consultative Document 3*, which was seen as possessing 'a certain anti-intellectual attitude towards the contribution of the social sciences to social work education . . . and a failure to appreciate the use of research findings' (Timms 1991: 207). One group of social work academics issued a publication in response to the consultative document in which they agreed with Timms' criticisms, but also saw in the document – notwithstanding its protestations to the contrary – CCETSW's ambition 'to impose centralist control, not only on social work education, but thereby, on thinking about social work itself' (University of Warwick 1978: Introduction).

At the conclusion of the consultation period, CCETSW stated: 'on the basis of the comments received, we do not believe that the Council has evidence that it should institute immediate and radical changes in any particular direction' (CCETSW 1983: 29).

1980s: consultation and change

Despite the cautious and inconclusive statement with which the 1970s consultation was terminated, the 1980s witnessed CCETSW moving on to propose major changes in social work education through a further period of review and consultation beginning in 1982. Central to its case for reforming social work education was CCETSW's view that the Certificate in Social Services (CSS) (an employment-based route to an alternative qualification, predominantly followed by residential and day care workers) and CQSW programmes were inadequate in respect of preparing social workers to undertake competently their statutory duties:

> Neither programme (CSS and CQSW) provides adequate education and training in length and depth for the increasingly complex demands imposed on social workers. Indeed, some of those holding existing qualifications who are given professional and statutory responsibility to protect the vulnerable have demonstrably lacked the knowledge and skills to do so.
>
> (CCETSW 1987: 10)

Although CCETSW levelled criticism at both CSS and CQSW programmes, once the Council had announced its intention to review social work education the Association of Directors of Social Services, whilst supporting CCETSW's wish to abolish the distinction between the two programmes, insisted that 'the best of CSS' should be adopted and adapted to the rules and requirements of the new social work qualification. Jones suggested that 'the best of CSS' was seen as 'the joint management of courses and the centrality accorded to practice competence in course design and student experience' (Jones 1989: 18).[1]

This second and protracted round of review resulted eventually in the publication of *Care for Tomorrow* (CCETSW 1987). This report constituted CCETSW's submission to government for an extra £40 million per annum in order to reform social work education. The report proposed that by the 1990s a new three-year Qualifying Diploma in Social Work would be launched to replace the existing CSS and CQSW programmes. In 1988 the government responded by rejecting CCETSW's *Care for Tomorrow* and withholding finance for the proposed three-year social work qualification. Instead, the government committed finance for the development of National Vocational Qualifications (NVQs) and Scottish Vocational Qualifications (SVQs) in social care, a two-year Diploma in Social Work and a Post-qualifying Framework.

The government's decision resulted in the publication of *Paper 30: Rules and Requirements for the Diploma in Social Work* (CCETSW 1989), with proposals to replace the CQSW and CSS programmes with a single qualification, the Diploma in Social Work. *Paper 30* marked a substantial shift from CCETSW's concerns in the 1970s and early 1980s in opening up consideration of the impact of discrimination and oppression in relation to social work and, in the process, placed in the mainstream of state deliberations themes, issues and debates which had previously existed predominantly in academic and to some extent in practice contexts.

A previous CCETSW publication, *Paper 20.6: Three Years and Different Routes. Council's Expectations and Intentions for Social Work Training*, had already proposed that the distinctive characteristics of social work resided in a social worker's commitment to 'challenging within his/her professional/employee role, racism, sexism, ageism and other institutional and oppressive attitudes which affect the delivery of service to the clients of his/her employing agency' (CCETSW 1986: 7). This theme was developed further in *Paper 30* (CCETSW 1989), in which CCETSW expressed its commitment to furthering anti-racist and anti-discriminatory practice, requiring qualifying social workers to combat discrimination based on age, gender, sexual orientation, class, disability, culture and religion (CCETSW 1989: 16).[2] In an introductory statement, CCETSW gave a definition of social work, consistent with this commitment:

> Social work promotes social welfare and responds to wider social needs, promoting equal opportunities for every age, gender, sexual preference, class, disability, race, culture and creed. Social work has the responsibility to protect the vulnerable and exercise authority under statute.
>
> (CCETSW 1989: 8)

This statement captures the tension between CCETSW's recognition of, and support for, social work as a state activity (the 'exercise of authority under statute') and its movement towards inclusion of a more critical and questioning form of social work seen as capable of promoting social welfare. In pursuing social work's more critical mandate, CCETSW's new requirements for social work programmes did not introduce a uniform curriculum that had to be followed. Instead, each programme's curriculum had to be adjudged by CCETSW as satisfying the national criteria of competence[3] that CCETSW had laid down. In parallel, the organisational structures for delivering social work programmes were standardised in a way that gave Social Services Departments the potential to secure a dominant voice in shaping and developing the curriculum of the programmes in which they were involved in partnership arrangements.[4]

1990s: a more modest mandate

Only minor revisions were made to *Paper 30* in its second edition (CCETSW 1991a). It continued to contain a mixture of questioning critical assertions alongside the acceptance of social work's role in fulfilling what were presented as its 'neutral' statutory obligations. These conflicting messages represented the compromise reached between a number of competing voices and viewpoints within CCETSW's membership (Humphries 1997: 645).

The more questioning critical assertions contained in *Paper 30* received extensive media coverage, leading to claims in national newspapers that social work and social work education had fallen prey to 'political correctness' (see, for example, Appleyard 1993; Phillips 1993) and to the emergence of more sustained critiques of this phenomenon (Dunant 1994). Substantial revisions were made to *Paper 30*, which re-emerged, with a more managerialist title, as *Assuring Quality in the Diploma in Social Work 1: Rules and Requirements* (CCETSW 1995a). At this stage, CCETSW's decision to remove anti-discriminatory practice as a central element of the qualification was undoubtedly influenced by central government concerns 'that social work education was far too preoccupied with "ologies and isms"' (Preston-Shoot 1996: 13). In the run-up to the appearance of the revised rules and requirements, Virginia Bottomley, then the Secretary of State for Health and previously a social worker, announced in a speech to the Conservative Local Government Conference that 'a National Core Curriculum for Social Work Training . . . will be no place for trendy theories or the theory that isms or ologies come before common sense and practical skills' (quoted in Preston-Shoot 1996: 13). As McLaughlin points out, 'such criticism did indeed have an effect on policy, with the appointment of Jeffrey Greenwood as chair of CCETSW in 1993. Whilst declaring his commitment to equal opportunities, Greenwood, in the *Independent* newspaper, also pledged to rid social work training of 'politically correct nonsense' (McLaughlin 2005: 295).

Clearly the revised agenda was leading in the direction of a less-of-this-academic-nonsense vocational training. This agenda was produced through a partnership between CCETSW and the Care Sector Consortium, in the Care Sector Consortium's role as the NVQ Occupational Standards Council for Health and Social Care. No doubt the relationship forged between the two organisations was central to the amplification of the importance of competence in social work by CCETSW, given that the Care Sector Consortium was charged with pursuing the competence agenda and was a potential threat to CCETSW's continued existence.

The review that had led to the publication of the revised rules and requirements for the Diploma in Social Work (DipSW) had five stated aims:

- to achieve contemporary relevance for the qualification in the context of changing needs, legislation and service delivery;
- to establish more consistent standards of outcome from Diploma in Social Work programmes;
- to provide a sound professional base for a career in social work, firmly located in higher education;
- to secure the place of the Diploma in Social Work in the continuum of qualifications;
- to promote flexible opportunities for access to education, training and qualification.

(CCETSW 1995b: 4)

CCETSW and the Care Sector Consortium employed consultants – the National Institute for Social Work and Mainframe – to develop 'national occupational standards' for social workers on which to base the revision of the statement of requirements for the DipSW. In order to develop the occupational standards, Mainframe used mapping techniques derived from functional analysis. These techniques were consistent with the government's general concern to place competence in learning and assessment at the centre of training for employment in a wide range of occupations, validated by nationally agreed occupational standards (CCETSW 1994). Mainframe's methodology appeared to have drawn heavily on that set out by the National Council for Vocational Qualifications (NCVQ 1988)[5] and involved a descending level of detail about social work: Units of Competence (Competencies); each Unit of Competence was sub-divided into Elements of Competence (Practice Requirements); Performance Indicators (Evidence Indicators) were then identified in the form of behaviours, which suggested whether each Element of Competence (Practice Requirement) was being met.

CCETSW maintained that in undertaking this process, there was 'extensive consultation, within the tight timetable requested by government' (CCETSW 1995b: 4), but the exercise was very different from previous consultations on the future of social work education. It was swift and prescriptive, with consultation on the detail of the proposals rather than debate about their general direction. Substantial revisions to the requirements for the Diploma in Social Work were approved by CCETSW's Council in February 1995 with the publication of *Assuring Quality in the Diploma in Social Work 1: Rules and Requirements* (CCETSW 1995a). The revisions were heralded as a great success by Tony Hall (then Director of CCETSW) who stated that 'no other profession defines so precisely and comprehensively the competencies required for its newly qualified practitioners' (CCETSW 1995b).

One of the major changes in *Assuring Quality in the Diploma in Social Work 1: Rules and Requirements* (1995a) was the move away from what was now depicted as the previous combative emphasis on anti-discriminatory practice, and anti-oppressive practice, and towards a more modest mandate for social work. This required students to develop knowledge and understanding of 'diversity and difference' (CCETSW 1995a: 9) and the assessment of students' competence was to be in terms of how they managed diversity, using an individualistic approach:

> This approach proclaims difference as essential in distinguishing need and prescribes responses to that need as a technical activity stripped of critical or radical ambition for change. It is essentially individualist, populist and pragmatic, and effectively operates to dissipate the politicisation of need by holding that everyone's needs are unique and special. The model holds no hope of intersectionality between groups as it serves essentially to fragment them, but it can accommodate notions of multi-oppression in that everyone is unique.
>
> (Williams 1999: 226)

This individualistic reading of CCETSW's emphasis on diversity[6] in *Assuring Quality in the Diploma in Social Work 1* (1995a) is reinforced by the fact that anti-discriminatory and anti-oppressive practice no longer appeared as requirements in any of the core competencies. The only point at which different sources and forms of oppression emerge is as part of the requirements for the qualification under the heading 'Ethics and Values in Social Work'. Here, it is stated that students should be aware of 'sources and forms of oppression, disadvantage and discrimination based on race, gender, religion, language, age, class, disability and being gay and lesbian, their impact at a structural and individual level, and strategies and actions to deal with them' (CCETSW 1995a: 23). It was stressed that any action on the part of students to 'counter discrimination, racism, disadvantage, inequality and injustice' should take account of 'strategies appropriate to role and context' (CCETSW 1995a: 18). Thus the tension that existed in the first and second editions of *Paper 30*, between the critical stance promoted by CCETSW and adherence to social work's statutory obligations, was now explicitly resolved in terms of the latter unambiguously having precedence in constraining the former. The inability to self-censor strategies appropriately in relation to 'role and context', as stated by CCETSW, would presumably indicate a student who was not yet competent.

Having considered the general historical trajectory of developments in social work education, we now turn to the impact of these developments in relation to mainstreaming gender.

Mainstreaming gender

Mainstreaming gender in social work education was part of a wider 'deployment of formerly radical themes in a new framework of regulation. The use of the term "empowerment" and the promotion of "anti-discriminatory" practice in social work illustrate this trend' (Langan 1998: 214). In this deployment, the terms 'anti-discriminatory practice' and 'anti-oppressive' practice appear to have been used interchangeably by CCETSW. Braye and Preston-Shoot have suggested that their meanings are different:

> [Anti-discriminatory practice] is reformist, challenging unfairness or inequity in how services are delivered or removing barriers to access . . . [It] seeks change, but within officially sanctioned rules, procedures and structures. Anti-oppressive practice is more radical, seeking a fundamental change in power structures and exploitative relationships which maintain inequality and oppression.
>
> (Braye and Preston-Shoot 1995: 107)

They regard anti-oppressive practice as more radical than anti-discriminatory practice because it acknowledges structural inequality and exploitation in legal, social and economic relationships and seeks a fundamental realignment of power relationships external to social work (Braye and Preston-Shoot 1995: 107). As a consequence, Preston-Shoot has argued that the solutions to problems proposed by the two forms of practice are qualitatively different:

> Anti-oppressive practice looks for solutions . . . based on analysis and intervention into the context, power, culture, organisational arrangements and structural relationships which impact on users and workers. This takes workers into social and political action, challenging and enabling users to challenge how they, and services 'for' them, have been perceived. This extends therefore, beyond the reformist agenda of anti-discriminatory practice which, whilst challenging unfairness or inequity, adopts a . . . problem solving perspective. It addresses prejudice, for instance in how services stereotype and marginalise people, but not the structures which maintain inequality.
>
> (Preston-Shoot 1995: 17)

Similarly, Phillipson also regards use of the term 'anti-discriminatory' as signifying practice which challenges unfairness, whereas 'anti-oppressive' practice 'works with a model of empowerment and liberation and requires a fundamental re-thinking of values, institutions and relationships' (Phillipson 1991: 14–15). Dalrymple and Burke see the law as the key to distinguishing anti-discriminatory practice from anti-oppressive practice:

> It is important to note this distinction [between anti-oppressive and anti-discriminatory practice], as all too often the terms are used interchangeably, without thought being given to the impact of both terms. For us, anti-oppressive practice is about minimising the power differences in society . . . Legislation which deals with issues of discrimination is specific and aimed at addressing unfair treatment faced, for example, by black people or women. Anti-discriminatory practice uses particular legislation to challenge the discrimination faced by some groups of people.
>
> (Dalrymple and Burke 1995: 3–4)

Dominelli has offered an expansive definition of anti-oppressive practice (AOP):

> A form of social work practice which addresses social divisions and structural inequalities in the work that is done with people whether they be users ('clients') or workers. AOP aims to provide more appropriate and sensitive services by responding to people's needs regardless of their social status. AOP embodies a person-centred philosophy; an egalitarian value system concerned with reducing the deleterious effects of structural inequalities upon people's lives; a methodology focusing on both process and outcome; and a way of structuring relationships between individuals that aims to empower users by reducing the negative effects of social hierarchies on their interaction and the work they do together.
>
> (Dominelli 1996:170–171)

CCETSW did not provide any such definitions with respect to its use of the terminology of 'anti-discriminatory' and 'anti-oppressive'. Nevertheless, *Paper 30* (CCETSW 1989, 1991a) required students to demonstrate anti-discriminatory/anti-oppressive practice and from then on the importance, or otherwise, of incorporating anti-discriminatory/anti-oppressive practice in social work became the subject of an increasingly polarised debate within social work education (Pell and Scott 1995). Some social work educators considered that the requirements around anti-discriminatory/anti-oppressive practice were 'too emphatic and pervasive, and ultimately self-defeating' (O'Hagan 1996: 17). Others argued they were necessary but insufficient as they stood (Statham and Carroll 1994). Despite such differences, a broad swathe of opinion within social work education regarded CCETSW's stance (CCETSW 1989, 1991a) as marking a move forward in requiring that students reached a 'national standard, albeit one which did not seem to be grounded in a particularly clear analysis of the nature of discrimination and oppression' (Mullender 1995: 61; and see Carter *et al.* 1992: 114). Thus, notwithstanding a lack of clarity, CCETSW was seen as taking anti-discriminatory/anti-oppressive practice seriously (Mullender 1995: 61) and giving its 'permission' for social work programmes to address issues of discrimination in identifying and changing ideologies, structures and practices that were oppressive (Cavanagh and Cree 1996: 2).

Within this overall emphasis on anti-discriminatory/anti-oppressive practice in the first and second editions of *Paper 30*, the requirements were at their most explicit in relation to 'race' and anti-racist practice. McLaughlin has suggested this was due, in part, to the pressure put on CCETSW by local authorities: 'For example, Hackney pressed CCETSW to address the inadequacies of much social work training which as it stood was ill-preparing students to work in an anti-racist manner' (McLaughlin 2005: 286). He cites Penketh as arguing that it was the 'rise of a counter-Thatcherite political opposition within the Labour party, local government and the equal opportunities community which created the "space" for CCETSW's anti-racist initiatives to develop' (Penketh quoted in McLaughlin 2005:

286). However the situation came about, some writers have concluded similarly that 'race' was 'given greater prominence, class, gender and disability much less so, whilst sexual orientation [was] overlooked completely' (Balen *et al*. 1993: 34; and see Wise 1995: 105). Although Lloyd and Degenhardt shared this view, they argued that *Paper 30* provided a framework within which it was possible to place gender on education and training agendas, enabling 'anti-sexism to be taken seriously' (Lloyd and Degenhardt 1996: 48).

Gender may have been less prominent than 'race' in CCETSW's publications but it was nevertheless placed in the mainstream of the developments CCETSW instigated. As we have seen, this was not the case as far as sexuality was concerned, with CCETSW adopting an agenda in relation to social divisions that ignored 'the complexities at play when considering sexual orientation' (Trotter and Gilchrist 1996: 64). It was suggested that the outcome of CCETSW directing programmes to 'tackle issues of inequality and structural oppression' was that 'race' and gender featured prominently on the curricula of many programmes but sexual orientation was treated tokenistically (Logan and Kershaw 1994: 62).

CCETSW's requirements as far as gender was concerned were set out as follows in *Paper 30* (1989 – and not amended in 1991 version):

- combat other forms of discrimination, based on age, gender, sexual orientation, class, disability, culture and creed (p. 10, para. 1.19);
- develop an awareness of the inter-relationship of the processes of structural oppression, race, class and gender (p. 16, para. 2.2.3);
- develop an understanding of gender issues and demonstrate anti-sexism in social work practice (p. 16, para. 2.2.3).

As already mentioned, in *Assuring Quality in the Diploma in Social Work 1: Rules and Requirements* (1995a), CCETSW's expectations in relation to anti-discriminatory/anti-oppressive practice were diminished and in their place came an emphasis on difference and diversity. As with the editions of *Paper 30*, the terminology used was not defined but the use of 'diversity' represented a move away from the previous focus on social divisions: 'Diversity is reflected through religion, ethnicity, culture, language, social status, family structures and lifestyle' (CCETSW 1995a: 28). A somewhat vague and general reference was made to 'sources and forms of oppression, disadvantage and discrimination and their impact at a structural level and individual level in society' (CCETSW 1995a: 20) and gender was mentioned only once. CCETSW required that students 'have knowledge and understanding of the diversity of individual lifestyles and communities in the UK; of the significance of poverty, racism, ill-health and disability; and of gender, social class and sexuality' (CCETSW 1995a: 9). Students were also considered as needing:

> Learning and practice experience in delivering social work services to children, families and communities in ways which are responsive to and respectful to

different faiths and cultural traditions, neither compounding disadvantage arising from race and social class, nor stigmatising people by reason of age, disability, illness, poverty or other difference.[7]

(CCETSW 1995a: 9)

After the introduction of the Diploma in Social Work in 1989, CCETSW produced a series of papers which were given the generic title *Improving Social Work Education and Training*. 'Race' and disability were the subject of publications in this series and the third publication was on gender issues and anti-sexist practice (Phillipson 1991). In the foreword, Rachael Pierce, Assistant Director of CCETSW, saw this publication as promoting and heightening awareness of gender issues on social work programmes.

It would be tempting to conclude that because discussion of gender was legitimated by CCETSW, women's experiences of state social work were now going to be firmly located within mainstream social work theory and practice. On the contrary, particularly in the context of the emphasis on competence (see below), 'while issues relating to gender and women [were] being incorporated into the mainstream of social work education, the space for feminist debate [was] closing off' (Graham 1992: 54), leading Graham to the conclusion that instead of there being more opportunities for feminists to develop challenging ways of thinking and practising feminism within social work, the new diploma's requirements were likely to produce less.

There seems to be some evidence to support this view. Although Phillipson saw her publication as the beginning of discussions on gender issues in social work education (Phillipson 1991: 5–6), four years later, as we have seen, gender slipped almost completely from the social work education agenda as contained in *Assuring Quality in the Diploma in Social Work 1: Rules and Requirements* (1995a). A process of mainstreaming seems to have been followed by a process of downgrading. This progression from mainstreaming to downgrading can be attributed to a number of problematic aspects in the developments that took place.

First, in the first and second editions of *Paper 30* people were seen as firmly located within specific social divisions. Although general references were made to interconnections between social divisions, the overall emphasis implied rigid allocation to particular categories (CCETSW 1989, 1991a). As a consequence, in seeking to follow CCETSW's requirements there was a tendency to search for forms of practice that relied on categories and procedures. In contrast, as we have seen, Graham challenged this 'search for anti-oppressive orthodoxy, a set of certain and fixed procedures for dealing with the complex issues raised by gender oppression' (Graham 1992: 56). Featherstone and Fawcett identified the pressure introduced by the Diploma in Social Work to retreat into orthodoxy, based on category construction, with students finding it hard to 'break out of the language of monoliths and accept understandings that are fluid and provisional' (Featherstone and Fawcett 1995b: 14).

The second difficulty with CCETSW's discussion of anti-discriminatory/anti-oppressive practice, particularly in the first and second editions of *Paper 30* (1989, 1991a), was that it was written in oppositional terms. CCETSW required students to '*challenge and confront* institutional and other forms of racism . . . and *combat* other forms of discrimination based on age, gender . . .' (CCETSW 1989: 10, my emphasis). Instead of the emphasis in CCETSW's later auto-critique on the 'tone' it adopted at this earlier stage (see above), perhaps the question to be asked is whether it is possible for students to challenge and combat discrimination and oppression, when they are firmly located within the context of state social work. Macey and Moxon commented that 'the realism of aiming to effect structural change from a grassroots level is generally questionable' (Macey and Moxon 1996: 308; and see Hugman 1996). Similarly Jordan has argued that statutory social work fits more easily into a liberal value framework and that the implication of CCETSW's reforms was that 'power, privilege and prejudice must be effectively challenged, but without upsetting the legal and moral foundation (economic and political individualism) on which they are built' (Jordan 1991: 5). As Webb argued, CCETSW's 'structural position [was] set four-square within what were once called the ideological state apparatuses: "surface" exhortations to repudiate discrimination [sat] alongside what [was] in effect an endorsement of neo-liberalism' (Webb 1996: 186).

A third problem that arose out of the way in which anti-discriminatory/anti-oppressive practice was discussed by CCETSW, was the implicit hierarchical ordering of oppressions mentioned earlier in the chapter, with 'race' being given greatest prominence by CCETSW and gender being given some attention, whereas sexuality was largely absent (Wise 1995; Dominelli 2002a: 162–163). In effect women's interests were downplayed overall and lesbian women's interests were then marginalised.

Fourth, there was always a tension within CCETSW's framework for the Diploma in Social Work between on the one hand a traditional liberal social work agenda, framed within the statutory context, and on the other hand a more radical agenda of promoting anti-discriminatory/anti-oppressive practice and confronting structural oppression. Logan and Kershaw concluded that 'a new imposed triad of radical, liberal and controlling agendas' was the context in which social work education in the 1990s was taking place (Logan and Kershaw 1994: 74). Traditionally, the values of social work were seen as 'clients' rights to dignity, privacy, confidentiality and choice and protection against abuse and violence' (CCETSW 1989: para. 2.2.2). Jordan has suggested that this traditional list of values 'has its roots in liberal ethics, market-minded politics, casework and law' (Jordan 1991: 5). These values fitted with the 'overall tone of the [*Paper 30*] requirements, with their priority on legal and procedural knowledge, and the application of technical skills' (Jordan 1991: 5). The radical agenda, on the other hand, was satirised by Webb as CCETSW having legislated concerning

which values social workers should hold, thereby determining the moral ground which practitioners should occupy. Possessed of the moral truth,

> CCETSW's high priests have sent out the word which all must follow and by which all will be judged, censured and watched.
>
> (Webb 1991: 151)

Fifth, the strengthening in the revised rules and requirements (CCETSW 1995a) of the emphasis on traditional social work values meant a move towards a more individualised way of working, with an emphasis on 'appropriate client–worker relationships' and 'contractual arrangements' (Dominelli 1996: 171). Dominelli suggested that in this context it was even harder for social workers to engage with the ramifications of organisational and structural oppression and they were just 'tinkering at the edges' (Dominelli 1996: 171). This argument was reinforced by Jones, who maintained that CCETSW had

> successfully managed a transformation of social work education where the concerns of the disadvantaged and marginalised, which should figure at the centre of social work education, have been swallowed up and have disappeared into the needs of the state agencies.
>
> (Jones 1995: 6)

In retrospect, the mainstreaming of gender seems to have been a mixed blessing at best in terms of promoting women's interests, and to have dwindled in significance as the social work education reforms were consolidated. To understand how the reforms placed further constraints on women social workers, we turn to a discussion of competence, followed by a consideration of partnership.

Competence

The term 'competence' was never adequately defined[8] in any of the three main publications about the Diploma in Social Work (CCETSW 1989; 1991a; 1995a). Nevertheless, competencies were seen as the key to establishing national criteria for standardising social work education and training. Competence was the foundation for the whole edifice on which the restructuring of social work education was built. Criticisms of the last edition of the rules and requirements for the Diploma in Social Work (CCETSW 1995a) came from many sources within social work education. At a national conference convened by social work educators the conclusion reached was that social work education had become driven by managerialism and had 'reached the end of the road: stuck in a cul-de-sac of regulation and conformity that stifles innovation and change' (Committee for Social Work Education and Policy, quoted in O'Hagan 1996: 3). The main criticism was that the emphasis had shifted to making competencies ('increasingly defined by legal statute and underpinned by bureaucratic procedure' [Jones 1993: 15]) relevant to the needs of social workers' employers, with the competence-based approach to social work being seen as: preparing practitioners for a market-driven environment (Dominelli 1997: 171), subordinating social work education to the concerns of management (Langan 1998: 216) and 'reinforcing managerial practices' (Adams 1998: 257).

Other arguments that were advanced against competence-based social work education were, first, that competence is a minimalist concept: 'It does not embrace the creative, intuitive and anti-oppressive nature of progressive work with people' (Issitt and Woodward 1992: 52); second, that competencies regulate the way in which social workers work (Jones 1993: 15; Humphries 1997: 656); third, that competencies encourage the development of superficial politically correct attitudes rather than a critical analysis of social work theories and practice (Cannan 1994/5: 11; Dominelli 1996: 162); and, finally, that competencies technicalise social work: 'Service delivery has become fragmented and reduced to discreetly identified parts or empirically stated technical competencies and quantifiable indicators' (Dominelli and Hoogvelt 1996: 52). Adams' pessimistic conclusion was that social workers were transformed from professionals to technicians as a result of the narrowing of ideas consistent with outcome-based activity, the focus on easily measurable aspects of people's performance and the concentration on techniques rather than critically reflective practice (Adams 1998). Taken together, these criticisms represented CCETSW as having subordinated social work education to the concerns of management, marginalised academic social science and elevated vocational training; the anti-discriminatory agenda was seen as offering a radical image for CCETSW, despite its being a highly conformist agency (Langan 1998: 216) and, it was argued, the radical gloss kept on board academics who might otherwise have been sceptical (Dominelli 1997: 162).

These arguments against a competence-based approach were grounded in a wider analysis that located the changes discussed thus far in social work education in the developments that had taken place generally within state social work (see Chapters 3 and 4), developments which were seen as having been the result of successive governmental regulation, surveillance and rationing (Jones 1995: 7; Dominelli 1996: 165; Harris 2003). Jones, for example, condemned CCETSW for yielding to 'employer pressure for a social work qualification which has been intellectually gutted to conform to their demands for a bureaucratically compliant workforce' represented in a 'shift towards an instrumental vocational assessment' (Jones 1993: 15). Brewster pointed to the minimal representation from social work educators on the CCETSW Council, which was responsible for making the shift to competence-based education, and the overwhelming representation of the interests of the managers of social work (Brewster 1992: 88–89). The presence of these managers was indicative of the shift towards a partnership model for social work education.

Partnership

As we saw earlier in this chapter, ideas about partnership between social work agencies and educational institutions had circulated since the late 1970s and had guided the gradual development of CCETSW policy (Payne 1994: 59). For example, in its report on the 1970s consultations referred to earlier in the chapter, CCETSW began to recognise the tensions that existed between higher education institutions and social work agencies, mainly centred around the planning and monitoring of placements and the disparity in views about social work skills and objectives (CCETSW 1983).

In parallel with its review of Certificate of Qualification in Social Work (CQSW) programmes, CCETSW set up the Certificate in Social Services (CSS). CSS was seen as embodying features that employers wanted; social work training that was tailored to meet the needs of the particular social work agency (CCETSW 1983). During the 1970s, employers had expressed their discontent with CQSW programmes, which were perceived as turning out students unable to do the job employers required of them and as populated by academics who were failing to inculcate students with familiarity with the law and respect for agency procedure (Dominelli 1997: 159–162; Jones 1999: 45). Increased negative media coverage of child abuse investigations resulted in the Association of Directors of Social Services complaining that social workers were no longer being equipped during their training to deal with child care issues (Cannan 1994/95: 12). CSS offered a different, partnership-based approach that began to address some of the short-comings about which employing agencies had complained.

The next stage in CCETSW's development of partnership came in the 1980s when CCETSW asked for comments from agencies on CQSW programmes. Although the response was mixed, CCETSW highlighted the fact that several agencies had emphasised 'the importance of harnessing together educational and agency resources, citing the value of their experience in planning CSS training through joint management committees, and contrasting this with their view that there was little opportunity for employers to exert influence on CQSW courses' (CCETSW 1983: 17). These employer pressures 'led CCETSW to emphasise collaboration between agencies and educational institutions in its formal decision to set up a new form of social work education, embracing both CSS and CQSW models' (Payne 1994: 61). In *Care for Tomorrow*, CCETSW stated that 'the primary aim of social work education and training is to produce a competent and accountable professional . . . educational institutions and agencies will be required to collaborate in the development and provision of the new programmes' (CCETSW 1987: 21).

The introduction of the Diploma in Social Work brought with it compulsory partnerships between educational institutions and social work agencies. CCETSW stated in *Paper 30* (CCETSW 1989) that the success of the Diploma in Social Work was dependent on 'collaboration between educational institutions and social services agencies' and that this was a central feature of CCETSW's new diploma (CCETSW 1990: 1). In order to support these collaborative partnerships, development money was made available from central government, although it was hoped that savings would be made through effective partnership arrangements. CCETSW's arguments in support of partnerships were:

- both field and academic learning are equally important and need to be closely integrated (CCETSW 1991b: 43);
- by having agency input, programmes could make the curriculum more relevant in preparing students for work in the personal social services (CCETSW 1987: 9);
- 'Partnerships are essential to achieve a high quality of education and training and to increasing the quantity of Diploma in Social Work holders that the personal social services require to meet client needs' (CCETSW 1991b: 43);
- more output would be achieved if resources were pooled (CCETSW 1991a: 43);
- improving quality means raising academic standards and making programmes more relevant. This requires 'programmes to be more responsive and permeable to contemporary social work practice' (CCETSW 1991b: 43).

Brewster argued that the emphasis on partnership, geared to employment-led training, was a smoke-screen: 'When CCETSW talks about employment-led training it should really be saying managerial-led training' (Brewster 1992: 88). Further, Brewster stated that new appointments to the advisory staff of CCETSW were drawn almost exclusively from the lower managerial positions in social work agencies. Managers also dominated representation on Diploma in Social Work Programmes' partnership bodies:

> This new agenda has altered the balance of autonomy hitherto enjoyed by social work education and instead through 'programme partnerships' has brought it into a direct and subordinate relationship if not with employers, then at least with the new manager cadres of the personal social services.
>
> (Webb 1996: 186)

Having provided an historical overview of the sweeping changes introduced into social work education by the Conservative governments, we now turn to the second wave of reform initiated by New Labour after it came to power in 1997. These reforms built on the Conservatives' first wave of reform by maintaining the emphasis on competence and partnership and moving decisively towards even more prescriptive approaches towards social work education.

Modernising the workforce

From 1997 onwards, social work education was swept up in New Labour's modernisation agenda (see Chapter 4), as four new organisations were set in place. CCETSW was abolished and the validation of social work courses shifted to the General Social Care Council (GSCC).[9] This was one aspect of the GSCC's declared mission to raise standards: 'The General Social Care Council exists to promote the highest standards of social care in England for the benefit and protection of people who use services and the wider public. Furthermore the GSCC defines itself as 'a guardian of standards . . . champion of the profession' (GSCC quoted in Horner 2003: 111). As part of its concern with standards, the GSCC produces codes of practice and manages the registration system for social workers. Entry to the register is dependent upon the applicant holding a social work qualification that demonstrates that s/he has met the occupational standards laid down for social work. The organisation responsible for these occupational standards, as part of New Labour's reforms, was the Training Organisation for the Personal Social Services (TOPSS). TOPSS has ceased to exist and, since April 2005, its responsibilities have been divided between Skills for Care, specifically concerned with the adult social care workforce, and the Children's Workforce Development Council, which has taken over workforce issues for children's services. The two bodies are envisaged as liaising closely and together are England's contributors to 'Skills for Care and Development', the UK-wide sector skills council for social care, children and young people. The aim of Skills for Care is 'to support employers in improving standards of care provision through training and development, workforce planning and workforce intelligence' (TOPSS 2005).

The third body to be established as part of the New Labour reforms was the Social Care Institute for Excellence (SCIE). SCIE's aim is 'to develop and promote knowledge about what works best in social care and then to disseminate knowledge through best practice guidance' (Department of Health, quoted in Horner 2003: 113). The fourth body, the National Care Standards Commission, was replaced in April 2004 by the Commission for Social Care Inspection, which 'brings together the work previously undertaken by the Social Services Inspectorate, the SSI/Audit Commission joint review team and the social care functions of the National Care Standards Commission' (CSCI 2005).

These organisational reforms were endorsed by Denise Platt, Chief Inspector of the Social Services Inspectorate:

> The new national infrastructure developments (the General Social Care Council, the Training Organisation for the Personal Social Services, the Social Care Institute for Excellence and the Commission for Social Care Inspection) will promote a common set of values and support people working in the whole social care sector across the full range of service user groups (adults and children).
>
> (SSI 2002: 2)

These developments framed the announcement by the Department of Health, in March 2001, that a three-year undergraduate social work course would be put in place from 2003, following consultation on *A Quality Strategy for Social Care* (Department of Health 2000 – see previous chapter). This three-year programme was to have a greater emphasis on practice learning and was to be based on a national curriculum (Department of Health 2000: para. 106) that addressed the occupational standards (drawn up by TOPSS), subject benchmarks (produced by the Quality Assurance Agency for Higher Education) and the GSCC's codes of practice. The Department of Health stated that the 'new degree level qualification must prepare social workers for the complex and demanding role that will be required of them' (Department of Health 2002: i).

The *National Occupational Standards of Social Work* were accorded a central position in the plans for the new social work qualification. They were published by TOPSS in May 2002 'to provide a baseline for identifying standards of practice which should be reached by a newly qualified social worker' (Department of Health 2002: 5). The Department of Health document *Requirements for Social Work Training* (2002) made clear that these standards would 'form the basis of the assessment of competence in practice . . . Practice is central to the new degree, with academic learning supporting practice, rather than the other way round' (2002: 1). In addition, providers were to 'ensure that the principles of valuing diversity and equalities awareness are integral to the teaching and learning of students' (2002: 3).

The *National Occupational Standards for Social Work* (TOPSS 2004) break down the key purpose and roles of social work. The key purpose of social work is taken from the definition put forward by the International Association of Schools of Social Work and the International Federation of Social Workers. Social work is defined as:

> a profession which promotes social change, problem solving in human relationships and the empowerment and liberation of people to enhance well-being. Utilising theories of human behaviour and social systems, social work intervenes at the points where people interact with their environments. Principles of human rights and social justice are fundamental to social work.
>
> (TOPSS 2004: 12)

The key roles of social work are broken down into units and elements and attached to each element are performance criteria. In total there are six key roles, 21 units, 77 elements and hundreds of performance criteria that make up the occupational standards for social work. Sources of discrimination emerge in relation to the knowledge base underpinning the occupational standards in so far as the wider context of social work is concerned, and under the section of the knowledge base on values and ethics practitioners are told they must 'value, recognise and respect the diversity, expertise and experience of individuals, families, carers, groups and communities by communicating in an open, accurate and understandable way' and 'understand and make use of strategies to challenge discrimination, disadvantage and other forms of inequality and injustice' (2004: 20). However, in the plethora of performance criteria, the only point at which social divisions emerge is under key role 2, unit 5, element 5.1. In one of the performance criteria for element 5.1, practitioners are requested to 'identify the nature of the relationship and the processes required to develop purposeful relationships, taking account of ethnicity, gender, age, disability, sectarianism and sexuality issues'

(2004: 27). In this performance criterion, social divisions are reduced from sets of power relations to something that should be borne in mind as a facet of a social worker's building of working relationships with service users. This individualistic approach to social divisions is the overriding emphasis in the occupational standards, with a shift to reducing anti-discriminatory and anti-oppressive practice to a limited focus on the social worker's personal ethical responsibilities and behaviour, as an aspect of 'key roles', with little prospect of, for example, sustained engagement with oppression on the basis of gender, as envisaged in the feminist social work literature:

- Work within professional, ethical and anti-discriminatory boundaries and practices when contacting individuals and organisations (key role 1, unit 1, element 1.2).
- Ensure that information provided addresses cultural, religious and other needs, is not discriminatory and is in an appropriate language and format (key role 1, unit 2, element 2.2).
- Work with groups to enable them to use an anti-oppressive framework within the group (key role 2, unit 8, element 8.1).
- Ensure any agreements are consistent with anti-discriminatory and inclusive practice (key role 4, unit 12, element 12.2).
- Review how your own practice and that of your colleagues counters disadvantage, discrimination and social exclusion (key role 5, unit 15, element 15.3).
- Review knowledge about issues of equality, fairness, access and anti-discriminatory practice and provision (key role 6, unit 18, element 18.3).
- Work sensitively when dealing with issues of diversity (key role 6, unit 19, element 19.1).
- Ensure that professional principles, codes and values are used in your practice, especially in relation to anti-discriminatory and inclusive practice (key role 6, unit 19, element 19.3).
- Identify ways in which your own service could reduce discrimination and promote equality and diversity for individuals (key role 6, unit 20, element 20.3).

As we have seen, the new social work courses were also expected to be responsive to the subject benchmark statement produced by the Quality Assurance Agency for Higher Education in terms of the academic standards that statement promotes. The QAA have stated that the subject benchmark statements 'provide a means for the academic community to provide general expectations about the "standards" for the award of qualifications at a given level and articulate the attributes and capabilities that those possessing such qualifications should be able to demonstrate' (QAA 2000: i). The benchmark statement for *Social Policy and Administration and Social Work* (QAA 2000), under the sub-heading 'defining principles', states that student social workers must learn to:

- recognise and work with the powerful links between intra-personal and inter-personal factors and the wider social, legal, economic, political and cultural context of people's lives;
- understand the impact of injustice, social inequalities and oppressive social relations;
- challenge constructively individual, institutional and structural discrimination.

(QAA 2000: 12)

Student social workers and practitioners are expected to know about:

- explanations of the links between definitional processes contributing to social differences (for example, social class, gender and ethnic differences) to the problems of inequality and differential need faced by service users;
- the nature of social work services in a diverse society with particular reference to concepts such as prejudice, inter-personal, institutional and structural discrimination, empowerment and anti-discriminatory practice.

(QAA 2000: 12–13)

All in all, social work courses are seen as enabling students to become 'account-able, reflective and self-critical' (QAA 2000: 12), with the benchmark statement being more forthright in its approach to issues of discrimination and oppression. The statement suggests that students should engage with such issues proactively, moving beyond an approach rooted solely in individualistic ethics and behaviour. However, this is hedged around with qualifications concerning accountability; the need for students to work in a 'transparent and responsible way, balancing autonomy with complex, multiple and sometimes contradictory accountabilities (for example, to different service users, employing agencies, professional bodies and wider society)' (QAA 2000: 12). In any case, at the end of the day, social work students' performance in practice learning is assessed against the occupational standards, not the QAA's subject benchmark statement.

The final referent for social work courses is the General Social Care Council's Codes of Practice for Employers of Social Care Workers and for Social Care Workers. The employers' code of practice sets out the responsibilities of employers for the regulation of social care workers. The code for employees provides a list of statements that 'describe the standards of professional conduct and practice' required of social care staff. Paragraphs 1.5, 1.6 and 5.6 emphasise the need for practitioners to promote equal opportunities, to respect diversity and difference and not to condone any unlawful or unjustifiable discrimination (GSCC 2004).

The intention lying behind the adoption of a national curriculum, derived from occupational standards and responsive to the subject benchmark statement and codes of practice, was made clear when Jacqui Smith, the then Health Minister, revealed the government's thinking about the nature of modern social work, when addressing the *Community Care Live* conference:

Social work is a very practical job. It is about protecting people and changing their lives, not about being able to give fluent and theoretical explanations of why they got into difficulties in the first place. New degree courses must ensure that theory and research directly informs and supports practice.

(quoted in Horner 2003: 3)

Similarly, in the foreword to the Department of Health's *Requirements for Social Work Training* (2002), Jacqui Smith stated that

The new award will require social workers to demonstrate their practical application of skills and knowledge and their ability to deliver a service that creates opportunities for service users . . . The emphasis must be on practice and the practical relevance of theory . . . This is not tinkering at the edges of social work training. This is a major shift in expectations of those providing the training and of those undertaking it.

(Department of Health 2002: i–ii)

Conclusion

By the various means reviewed in this chapter, the prominence of managerialism in state social work under Conservative and New Labour governments (see Chapter 4) can be seen as having been reproduced in social work education. Developments in this field have been regarded as 'an additional force in consolidating white male decision-making power' (Carter *et al.* 1992: 121), involving increased interference over what is taught, with the involvement by agencies representing increased managerial surveillance and supervision (Novak 1995: 5).

Nevertheless, the original agenda of CCETSW's *Paper 30* (CCETSW 1989) can be regarded, at least in part, as influenced by a range of interests, including those of women, in setting goals for addressing discrimination and oppression. Hugman has argued that the dominant view, from within various perspectives but nevertheless across this range of interests, was that social work would become increasingly incompetent and irrelevant unless it transformed its mandate in accordance with societal developments (Hugman 1996: 142–143).

However, the anti-discriminatory and anti-oppressive content imported into social work education was attacked by, amongst others, the Conservative government, which, as we have seen, ordered a review of *Paper 30*, based on a much narrower and functional analysis of the sort of social work needed to deliver objectives that the government considered to be acceptable. The end result was a technical, formulaic and prescriptive approach to students' behavioural performance in practice, geared to on-the-job competencies. Accountability to employers for educational provision, against the backcloth of managerialism (see Chapter 4), framed the social work tasks to be undertaken. The end result allowed Jones to claim that 'there is no comparable system of social work education in the world, which is so nationally uniform, uninspired and tailored so closely to the requirements of major state employers' (Jones 1996: 191).

CCETSW's limited capacity to act as a buffer against state encroachment was dispensed with easily, as fledgling alternative definitions of the goals of social work were overridden and state authority over social work education was asserted. Under New Labour, this state authority was consolidated first, by an intensified emphasis on competence, through the implementation of national occupational standards and their use as the basis for social work courses, and second, through the maintenance of partnership arrangements in the new guise of 'stakeholding'. These developments thus illustrate and underscore the extent to which, through another avenue (this time social work education), women social workers' 'technical autonomy' (their control over the means of undertaking social work) has been derived from, and constrained by, the ends of the state (see Chapter 3).

One element in the fleeting alternative definitions of social work put forward by CCETSW was the mainstreaming of gender as part of a wider agenda on anti-oppressive/anti-discriminatory practice. The faltering progress of this process of mainstreaming has been identified, together with some of the attendant difficulties, not least gender's location in competence-based and partnership-provided social work programmes in the first wave of reform and the petering out of the process with the introduction of national occupational standards in the second wave. Furthermore, the narrowing of scope implicit in the competence-based occupational standards approach has not been conducive to opening up egalitarian relationships with women service users, as proposed in the feminist social work literature (see Chapter 2).

These developments in social work education assist in contextualising women social workers' experiences. The particular relevance of this contextual strand is that the women social workers whose experiences are considered in the following chapters had been exposed to many of the developments in social work education that have been the subject of this chapter.

Chapter 6

Identities, identifications and stances

The preceding chapters have explored the contexts within which women social workers are located. Chapters 3 and 4 highlighted the centrality of the state context and the way in which that context constrains and shapes women social workers' practice. Chapter 5 reviewed key developments in social work education, focusing particularly on the place accorded to social divisions, including gender. Through these often contentious and contested developments in the contexts of women social workers' practice, they have been exposed to an agenda around anti-oppressive and anti-discriminatory practice. Chapters 1 and 2 considered how women social workers and their practice are positioned in the feminist social work literature. It became apparent that the overriding emphasis in the literature is on the possibility and desirability of women social workers identifying with the term 'feminist', as an identity that provides a stance from which to engage in egalitarian relationships with women service users that are aimed at their empowerment. This chapter explores women social workers' experiences of identities, identifications and stances, whilst Chapter 7 pursues egalitarian relationships and empowerment. Before turning to women social workers' experiences, the different approaches taken by writers to the ways in which terminology can represent particular identifications and stances are considered.

Identifications and stances

We have seen that the feminist social work literature has stressed the open and eclectic nature of the term 'feminist' (see Chapter 2). In contrast, we noted that Langan and Wise have argued for a different approach that moves the emphasis towards encompassing women's interests within a broader based anti-discriminatory social work. Langan has regarded this wider approach as capable of embracing manifold oppressions affecting the lives of women (Langan 1992a) and Wise has suggested that although such an approach can be informed by feminist analysis, together with analyses from other subjugated groups, this is different from the feminist social work literature's depiction of feminist social work (Wise 1995).

Some social work writers have stressed the importance of defining terms like 'anti-discriminatory' and 'anti-oppressive' with more precision and have suggested that social workers' choice of terms signifies the stance they adopt in their practice (Burke and Harrison 1998: 230). In essence, 'anti-discriminatory practice' has been seen as reformist and 'anti-oppressive practice' has been regarded as a more radical stance (Phillipson 1991; Thompson 1993; Preston-Shoot 1995; Braye and Preston-Shoot 1995; Dalrymple and Burke 1995; Burke and Harrison 1998; Dominelli 2002c). In contrast to these demands for terminological precision, Stanley (see Chapter 1) has been less confident about a dichotomous approach to definitions. She has stressed that women's usage of terms like 'women', 'feminism' and 'gender' differs, with the terms being used 'strategically' in some cases, including to signify a clear political stance, and 'accidentally' in other cases. She notes that for some women terminology is chosen after considerable thought, whereas for other women terms are used in a casual way (Stanley 1997: 11). hooks has gone further in arguing that 'feminism seems to be a term without any clear significance. The "anything goes" approach to the definition of the word has rendered it practically meaningless' (hooks quoted in Skeggs 2001: 43). Faced with this terminological ineptitude, Orme has counselled against adopting prescriptive approaches to what is seen as feminist practice because the use of codes and/or checklists can suggest that only certain practice is feminist: 'To encourage practitioners to follow codes uncritically can lead to conclusions that "it's feminist because I say so"' (Orme 2003: 136).

Having taken note of these different positions on possible identifications and stances, we now turn to women social workers' expression, in their own terms, of their identifications and the stances they adopted in relation to three areas. First, they were asked to give the terms they used in relation to social divisions. Second, they were asked to give their terms for work that addressed women's interests. Third, they were asked whether 'feminist' or 'feminist social worker' were terms they would use to describe themselves.

Social divisions

Anti-oppressive practice and anti-discriminatory practice

The women social workers were asked about the terms they used in relation to addressing social divisions and their reasons for their use of those terms. Eight of them chose the terms 'anti-oppressive practice' and 'anti-discriminatory practice'. Four (Ruth, Gita, Donna and Hilary) of the eight who selected both of these terms saw them as not having clear definitions: 'I feel comfortable with both terms' (Ruth).

Six of the social workers (Linda, Candy, Donna, Hilary, Theresa and Olive) regarded the terms as carrying messages about their identifications and stances in relation to social work. For two of them (Donna and Hilary), clarity of definition was not seen as essential to indicate that an identification and a stance was being adopted. Thus, Donna regarded 'anti-oppressive practice' as signifying practice that was 'more down to earth' and Hilary focused on the 'anti-' prefix as being more significant than either of the terms in their entirety because 'anti-' had strong, proactive connotations for her. For the other four (Linda, Theresa, Candy and Olive) of these six, the distinctions they made about how they used each of the terms were related to the specificity, or otherwise, of the practice described. Linda's and Candy's distinction between the two terms lay in their usefulness in clarifying whether general or specific practice was under consideration. They saw 'anti-oppressive practice' as a more general term than 'anti-discriminatory practice'. Theresa used 'anti-oppressive' to indicate support for oppressed groups and 'anti-discriminatory' to refer to particular pieces of work, as did Linda. Olive reserved use of 'anti-oppressive practice' for the institutional level and used 'anti-discriminatory' to identify personal dimensions and groups experiencing discrimination. Although the definitions of these four participants were not uniform, they were the only participants who made distinctions about the usage of 'anti-oppressive' and 'anti-discriminatory' and, in doing so, they came closest to the position of the social work writers who have argued for such distinctions to be made (see previous section). All four had been closely involved in developments in social work education in a number of different roles and so might have been exposed to more debate around the use of terminology than the other four participants in this group.

Anti-oppressive practice

Of the nine women social workers who preferred to use the term 'anti-oppressive', eight of them (Helen, Liza, Amy, Elsie, Cindy, Janis, Zina and Denise) valued the term because of the breadth of issues they saw it as encompassing: '"Anti-oppressive practice" is about not oppressing any client. I feel comfortable with this term' (Zina). In addition, Angela saw the 'anti-' prefix as signifying the adoption of a proactive stance and Janis suggested that the term 'anti-oppressive practice' highlighted being personally implicated in discrimination and the significance of power relations. Their views concur with that of Dominelli, who argues that 'anti-oppressive practice goes beyond forms of social work that focus on a specific social division, e.g. anti-racist social work and feminist social work, to address all dimensions of oppression that impact on a person, and consider the complexities of the social relationships in which both clients and workers are embedded and within which they exercise agency, or their power to achieve their particular objectives' (Dominelli 2002c: 182).

Anti-discriminatory practice

Two (Gaye and Anita) of the three women social workers who used the term 'anti-discriminatory' valued it for the same reason that eight of those who used 'anti-oppressive' valued that term, namely for the breadth of issues 'anti-discriminatory' was regarded as encompassing: '"Anti-discriminatory practice" covers everything' (Anita). Iris regarded the term as indicating a commitment to countering the Social Services Department being implicated in discrimination and Gaye saw it as more political and proactive than other terms.

Difficulties in identifying terms

Four of the women social workers commented on the difficulty they had in identifying a term that reflected their stance towards social divisions. Although they all went on to state a preference for one or more terms, they indicated that their choice was somewhat arbitrary: 'I sat on a training day not very long ago, trying to tease out the difference between these terms, "anti-oppressive", "anti-discriminatory", "equal opportunities" and I don't think I was very much the wiser at the end of the day' (Gita).

Regardless of the terms that they themselves would want to use to represent their identifications and stances in social work, four women social workers from the same Social Services Department noted that in their day-to-day work they had to comply with a departmental stricture to use 'non-discriminatory'. Similarly, two of the women social workers from another Social Services Department stated that 'equal opportunities' was a term that they would have to use. For example, Olive highlighted the need to practise within the department's policy of 'promoting anti-discriminatory practice in line with the Social Services Department's Equal Opportunities Policy' and Candy thought the term 'equal opportunities' was in official use: '"Equal opportunities" is seen to incorporate all the social divisions, speaking to service users and workers'. Mission statements for particular teams, formulated within the equal opportunities policy, were considered to be influential in relation to women social workers' practice:

> Every team has to develop their own Equal Opportunities Statements. I suppose, actually, 'equal opportunities' is used more than 'anti-discriminatory' or 'anti-oppressive', and so we have this statement that we worked on last year, when the team split up into various groups to look at issues like gender and staffing, equal opportunities in relation to staff, service users, people with disabilities and then from those working parties, the team's Equal Opportunities Statement was formulated.
>
> (Candy)

When given a free choice, there was little consistency or pattern in the usage of different terms by women social workers, other than two of their workplace locations constraining them to use 'official' terminology, rather than their preferred terms. This could be regarded as emerging from, and reflecting, a more general state of imprecision in definitions of terminology and/or it could be that the terms were invested with specific and individual meanings by the women social workers. Of particular significance is that, when given a free choice, none of the terms selected by the women social workers mentioned 'gender', 'women' or 'feminist' at any stage in the discussion. This would seem to suggest that this group of women social workers adopted terminology in their day-to-day work that encompassed a range of social divisions, a position closer to that suggested by Langan and Wise than that of the mainstream feminist social work literature (see Chapter 1).

Women's interests

In order to elicit the specific identifications and stances of women social workers in relation to addressing the interests of women, within these broader practice stances, the women social workers' responses along that dimension are now presented.

Helen and Janis saw the term 'anti-oppressive practice' as embracing work in relation to any social division and regarded it as unnecessary to be more specific about addressing women's interests: 'All my work falls under "anti-oppressive practice". I would class any kind of work as "anti-oppressive practice"' (Helen).

Although six of the women social workers used various terms that laid the stress on 'women' ('women's perspectives', 'women-centred', 'womanism' 'women's issues'), the reasons given for their usage were all concerned with seeking over-arching terms which were inclusive of all women or all issues impacting on women. Thus, Olive, in passing, dismissed 'feminism' as a term because she considered it excluded some women:

> Well I generally try and use 'women-centred' or 'womanism', simply because for me these terms cover all women, regardless of what woman you are, whether you are a black woman, a disabled woman, a middle-class woman, whereas some of the other terms like 'feminism' are very exclusive of certain groups of women, whereas for me womanism suggests that you look at things from a woman's point of view.
>
> (Olive)

Olive's position concurs with that of Ang (1995), who has suggested that feminism

> can never ever be an encompassing home for all women, not just because different groups of women have different and sometimes conflicting inter-ests, but, more radically, because for many groups of 'other' women other interests, other identifications are sometimes more important and politically pressing than, or even incompatible with, those related to their being women.
>
> (Ang 1995: 73)

Eight of the women social workers used terms that referred to 'gender' ('gender issues' and 'gender awareness'). Iris and Cindy opted for 'gender issues' and 'gender awareness' respectively in order to indicate a wish to move beyond a concern only with women. For the remainder, the reasons they gave for their use of their particular terms remained vague.

Gaye and Amy preferred the term 'sexism' to indicate oppression against women, with the rider from Amy that the sexism would have to be 'overt' in order to be so described. Angela and Candy opted for the term 'feminist', on the basis of self-identification and alignment with the term.

Although the feminist social work literature has taken an eclectic approach to the term 'feminist' (see Chapter 1), 'feminist' was only chosen by two of the women social workers, when asked for a term to describe their identification and stance in relation to addressing women's interests. The remainder of the women social workers had a preference for terms that they regarded as inclusive and were connected to 'women', 'gender' and 'sexism'. This, again, suggests a commitment to a broader anti-discriminatory approach. Indeed, in the case of two of the women social workers, they did not see the necessity to move beyond the term 'anti-oppressive practice' and simply repeated its use in relation to women.

'Feminist'

As we have seen, only two of the women social workers used 'feminist' to refer to their stance in relation to addressing the interests of women. All of the women social workers were subsequently asked if they would describe themselves as 'feminist'.

Eleven of the women social workers said that they would describe themselves as feminist. Six did not consider themselves as 'feminist' but said that they drew on feminist principles in social work. Three did not consider themselves as 'feminist'. The eleven women social workers who described themselves as 'feminist' were sub-divided into two groups. Two of the women social workers within the 'feminist' group had designated themselves as 'feminist' earlier in their interviews in response to discussion about their identifications and stances in their work with women. The remaining nine, despite their willingness to describe themselves as 'feminist', indicated difficulties they had with the term in relation to what it meant to them and how it was perceived by others. In other words, although identifying themselves as 'feminist', they did not align themselves with the term unproblematically and introduced qualifications about their use of the term. Four stances were identified.

Feminist

The first grouping contained the two women social workers who, unprompted, had identified and aligned themselves with 'feminist':

> I call myself a feminist. I mean, there are probably quite a few different definitions. In terms of, in that I work towards getting sort of women's issues on the agenda, I think it is a personal and a political thing, definitely. I mean, in terms of being aware of issues around women and trying to empower women in their lives, that's how I would see myself as a feminist.
>
> (Candy)

> I would describe myself as a radical feminist. I am a lesbian and a feminist. I am committed to being visible as a lesbian because I believe that maintaining one's identity in comfort is a basic human right.
>
> (Angela)

Feminist with reservations

The second grouping consisted of nine practitioners who considered themselves to be 'feminist' because they drew on feminist principles in social work. They saw feminist principles in social work as being concerned with valuing and validating women service users:

> I would see myself as feminist within certain frameworks, as being more a person who is interested in women being valued.
>
> (Theresa)

> I do think that women's views are very valid, that women are very oppressed and they get quite a bad deal, in a lot of aspects of our society, and that we've got to stand up for that and we've got to be heard.
>
> (Ruth)

> The positive bits for me within feminism are the bits that actually enable value to be given to women's experiences.
>
> (Linda)

However, this grouping did have reservations and qualifications about the term 'feminist', particularly in wanting to distance themselves from any political connotations that 'feminist' might have:

> I mean the first time someone said to me, I think you adopt a very feminist approach, I was sort of, 'Oh! I'm not a feminist', you know, and I think that's because of some of the connotations that are around, about feminism and for me being 'woman-centred' doesn't carry those negative connotations and so it allows me to be a feminist but in a way that I actually find acceptable.
>
> (Linda)

> I'm wary of the word feminist but I think I feel comfortable with it myself because in life roles generally, I'm a woman first and a social worker next or whatever, you know? So I feel comfortable in that I am a feminist because I am female and I work from that point of view. What I am wary of is the feminist with a capital 'F', and what other people think about that.
>
> (Elsie)

Four of this grouping of women social workers mentioned the word 'radical' as a connotation of 'feminist' with which they did not wish to be associated:

I would link myself more to valuing women than seeing myself as being oppressed by men, so it's not sort of radical feminism. I draw on feminist principles but not radical feminism.

(Theresa)

I feel that I am a feminist and yet I'm aware that there will be people who are quite radically feminist who would think that I'm not. So I think because of my feelings about valuing women that, to me, makes me a feminist, but I appreciate that, to other people, that that isn't sufficient and that hasn't gone far enough, just sort of general principles, and general values.

(Ruth)

The negative bits, I suppose, are the sort of bra-burning mob radical bits, because I don't see myself as a radical.

(Linda)

I don't agree with radical feminism. It becomes competitive and loses its meaning.

(Donna)

Two others, although designating themselves as 'feminist', said they were covertly so, being concerned about identifying themselves publicly as 'feminist':

I would say I am a feminist, but I'm not, sort of, an overt one I suppose. I mean, I've tried to read feminist theoretical stuff but I find there is a particular language that's used in feminist books which I find really hard going.

(Amy)

I think I'd see myself as a feminist but I don't think I would tell people I was a feminist as such.

(Gaye)

Not feminist but drew on feminist principles

The third grouping consisted of five women social workers who did not consider themselves to be 'feminist' but said that they drew on feminist principles in social work. Although she saw herself as drawing on feminist principles, Cindy used the term 'gender awareness' to describe her work and considered that this term was better suited to her work setting and her involvement in the recruitment, selection, training and support of foster carers. She said that she consciously avoided the term 'feminist', as she considered it to be too complex and political for work with foster carers:

When we're looking at issues of placement, there may well be issues with regard to males. I'd probably use the word 'gender'. There's something about it not being so political. And also I think, having said that, I think, even with using the word 'gender', you need to be clear about what you're saying, but the word 'feminist' is probably the more complex.

(Cindy)

Janis similarly distanced herself from the term 'feminist'. However, she found aspects of feminist research helpful in practice:

I would not call myself a feminist, but I very much approve of feminist principles, the equality of women and equality of opportunity, so if it is relevant I would look at feminist perspectives. I mean, particularly working with young people like anorexics, where the feminist research is quite useful.

(Janis)

Not feminist

The last grouping contained four women social workers, who did not consider themselves to be 'feminist' and did not see themselves as drawing on 'feminist principles'. Two of them associated their standpoints either with feeling that they had not experienced oppression as women or with being concerned that feminism could oppress men:

I've never thought of myself as a feminist. I never had a sort of bent towards feminism, I think, because the passion wasn't there because it had never meant that much to me. I haven't had to fight for my rights as a female.

(Gita)

I'll be totally frank. I believe, although it's probably not a popular view, especially not with feminists, that it doesn't help to have a label as a 'feminist' in that way. I see myself as equal to everybody else and them equal to me and I know that women have been oppressed for a long time, kept down, but I don't particularly want to perpetuate a similar oppression on men, you know. I still take the view that I'm equal and that people are equal to me.

(Helen)

The other two women social workers had clear views on the oppression women experienced but had anxieties about feminist social work not recognising the realities of women service users' situations and thereby putting women service users in a difficult position:

I don't find a feminist perspective helpful. I find it difficult because feminist social work puts women service users in difficult positions, giving them options which are not realistic. So, I'm a realist.

(Liza)

Similarly, for Olive, as we saw earlier, the term 'feminist' was problematic because she thought it was addressed to white middle-class women and was unrealistic about the choices service users had available to them:

> Well for me feminism doesn't actually address issues around black women and working class women necessarily, because it somehow suggests that women have choices and for many of the women that we work with, in social services, they have very few choices, so I'd rather use a 'woman-centred' approach where I can look at women in whatever situation that woman finds herself to be in, rather than looking at feminist perspectives, which I think exclude black women and working-class women particularly, and I think women with disabilities.
>
> (Olive)

In relation to the term 'feminist', at one end of the continuum of responses are two women social workers who regarded themselves, unprompted, as 'feminist'. At the other end of the continuum are four women social workers who rejected the term. Of the remaining fourteen, five women social workers also did not regard themselves as 'feminist' but did not reject the term completely because they found 'feminist' principles and research useful. The final nine women social workers regarded themselves as 'feminist' but had reservations about the use of the term. On the one hand, the stances of these fourteen women social workers in relation to 'feminist' could indicate the failure of eclectic strategy proposed by the feminist social work literature (see Chapter 1), given the level of ambivalence that they expressed. On the other hand, these women social workers' stances could be regarded as indications of the success of this strategy, namely that 'feminist' principles had some appeal beyond the ranks of (in this case two) women social workers who regard themselves as unambiguously 'feminist', even extending their appeal to women social workers who state that they are not 'feminist'. What is clear is that for the majority of the women social workers, their engagement with what 'feminist' meant, fed into a broader anti-discriminatory agenda, as suggested by Wise and Langan, rather than steering them towards feminist social work as portrayed by the mainstream feminist social work literature (see Chapter 1).

Conclusion

In this chapter, we have seen that for all of the women social workers their identifications and stances in relation to seeking to counter the impact of social divisions on service users' lives through social work were either 'anti-oppressive practice', 'anti-discriminatory practice' or a combination of the two. As we noted, the lack of consistency or pattern in the use of different terms by the women social workers could be regarded as emerging from, and reflecting, a more general state of imprecision in definitions of terminology (see Chapter 1) and/or it could be that the terms were invested with specific and individual meanings by the women social workers. Either way, the women social workers did see themselves as engaged in anti-discriminatory and/or anti-oppressive practice, with some of them having to modify their preferred terms in the workplace in order to comply with the terminology of their employing departments.

In contrast, in relation to aligning themselves with a 'feminist' identity, none of the women social workers identified with the stance that is proposed in the feminist social work literature in the sense of embracing a feminist identity that infused all aspects of their experiences in social work. For most of these women social workers, feminism seemed to be associated with whatever aspect of their practice could be seen as empowering women (see Egeland 2004: 182). Only two of the women social workers, Candy and Angela, who had the strongest identification with the term 'feminist', could be seen as representing the position put forward by Langan and Wise, which was recapitulated at the beginning of the chapter. The stance of these two women social workers was to regard their feminist identification as contributing to their wider commitment to anti-oppressive/anti-discriminatory practice (AOP/ADP). This can be demonstrated by tracking their pathways from their identification with the term 'feminist', through the (same) term that they chose to identify their practice with women, to the terms they used to indicate their stances in social work (Figure 6.1). At the other end of the continuum of responses were four women social workers who did not identify themselves with the term 'feminist' (Figure 6.2).

Feminist	>	**Practice with women**	>	**Social work**
Candy	>	Feminist	>	ADP and AOP
Angela	>	Feminist	>	AOP

Figure 6.1 Pathways for 'feminist'.

Not feminist	>	**Practice with women**	>	**Social work**
Helen	>	AOP	>	AOP
Gita	>	Gender	>	ADP and AOP
Liza	>	Women	>	AOP
Olive	>	Women	>	ADP and AOP

Figure 6.2 Pathways for 'not feminist'.

Helen saw anti-oppressive practice as encompassing work with women and did not see the need to differentiate her work with women from her work with service users more generally. Despite also rejecting the term 'feminist', Liza, Gita and Olive did differentiate their stance in relation to work with women from their overall stance in social work, through identification with terms which refer to 'women' or 'gender'.

In the middle of the continuum of responses, the bulk (14) of the women social workers were in some measure seeking to use feminism, or principles derived from it, albeit with varying degrees of commitment to the term 'feminist'. In addition, for many of these women social workers 'feminist' was regarded with suspicion or reservation as a term of self-identification but had stronger support as a term, or as a set of principles, which had something to offer to their commitment to women, which existed in varying forms and to varying degrees, as part of their anti-oppressive/anti-discriminatory stances in social work (Figures 6.3 and 6.4). They reflected the 'I'm not a feminist but' stance, which

> is a way of speaking feminism without making an identification with it. It may display a refusal to be fixed as feminist, but may also be a sign of the inability to position oneself as feminist because of confusing and contradictory messages about what feminism actually is.
>
> (Griffin quoted in Skeggs 2001: 142)

'Feminist' with reservations	>	Practice with women	>	Social work
Denise	>	Women	>	AOP
Donna	>	Women	>	ADP and AOP
Elsie	>	Women	>	AOP
Iris	>	Gender	>	ADP
Theresa	>	Gender	>	ADP and AOP
Anita	>	Gender	>	ADP
Ruth	>	Gender	>	ADP and AOP
Gaye	>	Sexism	>	ADP
Amy	>	Sexism	>	AOP

Figure 6.3 Pathways for 'feminist with reservations'.

Not feminist/ feminist principles	>	Practice with women	>	Social work
Cindy	>	Gender	>	AOP
Janis	>	AOP	>	AOP
Linda	>	Women	>	ADP and AOP
Hilary	>	Gender	>	ADP and AOP
Zina	>	Gender	>	AOP

Figure 6.4 Pathways for 'not feminist but use feminist principles'.

Tracking these pathways reinforces the lack of evidence concerning the women social workers primarily aligning themselves with feminist identity, as suggested by the mainstream feminist social work literature. The different identifications and stances revealed in this chapter suggest that 'the feminist dream of a common language' (Haraway quoted in Lennon and Whitford 1995: 215) was not being realised amongst these women social workers and, instead, 'a multiplicity of approaches, positions, and strategies' were in evidence (Kemp and Squires 1997: 3), with 'feminist' as 'a contested space, a category under continual dispute and negotiation' (Griffin quoted in Skeggs 2001: 89). This chapter further suggests that Langan's and Wise's arguments for adopting a broader based anti-discriminatory practice best capture the often partial ways in which the women social workers drew on aspects of what they saw as 'feminist' in their wider anti-oppressive/anti-discriminatory stances. How these stances were translated into practice is the subject of the next chapter.

Chapter 7

Egalitarian relationships and empowerment in practice

Chapter 6 presented women social workers' experiences of identifications and stances as being much less clearly aligned with feminist identity than their depiction in the mainstream feminist social work literature (see Chapter 1). The women social workers' responses indicated a range of identifications and stances, the majority of which were more ambiguous and ambivalent than the feminist social work literature's identification and stance. Having explored women social workers' experiences of feminist identity, in this chapter we begin by turning to their experiences of egalitarian relationships. The feminist social work literature (see Chapter 2) has suggested that the shared experience of oppression between women provides the basis for such relationships, whereas Wise (1995, see Chapter 2) has questioned this. Having considered women social workers' experiences of egalitarian relationships and empowerment, the chapter concludes by examining how women's interests were addressed in the particular settings within which the women social workers were employed.

Egalitarian relationships

With service users

The women social workers identified the possibility of shared experience but were hesitant to stress this in case it overlooked differences between service users:

> I think every woman's situation is going to be different and whatever those differences they need to be respected and taken account of and I think that is particularly true of carers, you know. Every carer that I've had, they need different opportunities maybe to have their own space or to get support. We can't assume that they're all oppressed in the same sort of way, but there will be certain aspects of their life experience where there will be some areas of commonality. There's no doubt about that.
>
> (Theresa)

I've had women with post-natal depression in a group and they find it's not just them, other women feel very much the same. Although their individual problems are different, the feelings are similar.

(Elsie)

When it came to women social workers' relationships with women service users, the majority of the women social workers moved from hesitancy to certainty and all but two of them maintained that egalitarian relationships were not possible:

I don't think there can be equality between myself and service users. OK, we are both women, but that's as far as it goes.

(Iris)

I believe that it is impossible to have an equal relationship with service users. It would be unwise to instil a false sense of security or trust. If social workers evoke that to get families to do what they want, then it's bad practice. You must be honest about your role.

(Amy)

If you are meeting people you work with in a neutral setting and are not meeting them because of your job, then there could be some equality, but in a social work role, there is no equality whatsoever.

(Linda)

Only two of the women social workers countenanced even the possibility of more egalitarian relationships with women service users. One of them was Denise, but she thought that the combination of the professional role she occupied and her sexuality made it difficult for her to realise her wish to work in a more egalitarian way:

That stuff about we're all in this together because we have things in common. I try and work towards that to some extent, but it is difficult, partly because I am a lesbian and I have difficulty empathising with heterosexual women, and partly to do with my professional role. I don't think I'm that worked out in this area.

(Denise)

Candy came closest to the position set out in the feminist social work literature, as we will see when we move on to discuss empowerment later in the chapter.

With students

Given that the women social workers thought that there was little possibility of more egalitarian relationships with women service users, I explored their experiences of working with student social workers in their role as practice teachers.

(Given that the power relationship and social distance between practice teachers and students was likely to be less than that between social workers and service users, if the lack of evidence of woman-to-woman egalitarian relationships with service users was carried through into woman-to-woman relationships with students that might serve to confirm, by implication, the difficulty of realising woman-to-woman relationships on an egalitarian footing with women service users.) The responses fell into three groupings.

In the first grouping, five of the women social workers were wary of assuming that shared experience was a basis from which to work with women students:

> I don't work from the standpoint of automatically having things in common with female[1] students. It's just, you know, we're going to be two people here with different experiences, some of which we can share, some of which I can guide and assist, but I don't make that overall assumption that we have things in common. It varies with the students. I mean I've had male students who've been incredibly aware and sensitive to women's issues and issues around women's discrimination and oppression particularly. Oh yes, some of them have produced some brilliant written work around it in cases, and are able to look at things. I mean I'd find it difficult to say they could look at it from a feminist perspective, but they would take a feminist approach to analyse the whole situation.
>
> (Theresa)

What Theresa moved quickly on to stressing here was the role she occupied as a practice teacher and the way in which that role guides her responses to, and identifications with, women students. These women social workers took this as axiomatic and emphasised their role in teaching women students about oppression, rather than assuming a starting point in their shared experiences as women:

> I suppose I've learnt from looking at anti-racist practice that you can't assume that because someone is black that they have got racism sussed and similarly I can't assume that because someone is a woman that they have got woman-centredness, or whatever we want to call it, sussed because it will be about differential experiences and I will have to recognise that for some women they will have not have recognised – I find it difficult to believe that no woman has actually not experienced oppression – but they will certainly not have recognised the subtle ways in which they have been oppressed and I can't make those assumptions, so we have got to spend some time testing that out before we might have some common ground, some common understanding of the words that we're using. I think most students would say that with me placements are quite heavy because it is about unpacking a whole load of language and not just making assumptions that because we use a word that we both experience that word in the same way, even if we're both women.
>
> (Linda)

At the same time, these women social workers were at pains to stress that teaching about oppression should not be didactic; rather, students were seen as needing to find their own way to understandings of their position in social work. A black woman social worker stated that she was 'careful not to make assumptions about the level of students' awareness in terms of race and gender issues', regardless of a student's gender or ethnic origin. She described herself as actively resisting identification with students, even when she might share experiences with them as black women:

> It's actually trying to locate their strengths and trying to pull that out, build on that and actually trying to say to myself, well I might have been in that position once, but not actually using those words because its kind of dangerous, if I'm saying, 'well, if I were you, this is what I would do'. I really don't ever want to say that, so I really avoid saying that. But at the same time, trying to get the message over that I understand where they are coming from and how hard it is, and that, in terms of the double jeopardy effect, and perhaps being a woman, and a black woman, what that might mean, and the amount of internalised racism that you have actually got inside and how you can actually do some searching and perhaps get rid of some of that. So I think perhaps I give a lot more of personal resources within that kind of situation.
>
> (Olive)

Another black woman social worker went further than Olive and saw the assumption of shared experience on the part of black women students as problematic:

> I have perhaps run into more difficulties with black students than I have ever with white students. There's no reasons, no set reasons, why. This is just purely speculation on my part really. I guess when a white woman student comes, they see me as a black practice teacher and they think, 'yeah, we've got to get it right here'. Whereas a black woman student, and maybe its unfair for me to say, but it certainly has come across in the interactions that's gone on, thinks that it's going to be an easy ride, it's going to be black-on-black basically.
>
> (Hilary)

Ann explained how her view on shared experience as the basis for more egalitarian relationships with women students had shifted, following difficulties she had encountered when she provided a placement for a particular student who, like her, was lesbian:

> This was not an arranged match, just a fluke. I was delighted about it. This, I thought, was a placement match made in heaven. Neither of us would face homophobia in our dealings with one another and we would be able to support one another's choice about being visible and un-closeted. The student, though,

had different ideas about it. She chose not to be out except to me, not even to colleagues in the same team room. This forced me into a conspiracy of silence that I found hard to deal with. I also had to deal with my own disappointment about it and there were some important lessons for me to learn about people not being here to live up to my expectations, and about me making presumptions. She also tried to get me to collude with her on the basis of our both being gay. For example she demanded the right to take her partner to work each morning, even though this made her very late. I think she felt that as gay people we should stick by each other, a 'we're-both-in-this-together' kind of approach. The placement that should have been the match made in heaven turned out to be a bit hellish.

(Angela)

In the second grouping, three women social workers saw shared experiences with women students as the basis for relationships that were more egalitarian than those they had with men students:

I do feel that the women students and I understand each other on a different level, because we are both women. Much easier, much better, than men.

(Denise)

I'm starting with, in my mind, the possibility of oppressions on her and on me, at a personal level. Then as a case study, or piece of intervention comes up, then I'd be looking at that particular case. My experience with female students is in many respects very different because we are both women. It feels very easy to enable a female student to draw on her own experiences as a woman in order to empathise with clients and help them understand society's pressures and expectations.

(Gaye)

When I had a female student, it was just so much easier because there was so much that I assumed she already knew just because we were both women. If the student is a woman, I start from a different perspective, maybe still about mental health, but I talk to her as one woman to another woman, and talk to her about a woman's perception of the world, so that she could maybe link it into her own experiences and perception of her position in the world, in life.

(Elsie)

The final grouping brings together examples of responses from women social workers who mentioned difficulties in working with men students. These difficulties were experienced in a number of ways. First, there was difficulty in trying to get men students to have views of women service users' problems that were seen as acceptable by the women social workers in their role as practice teachers:

It was only after having a female student that I realised how much harder I had had to work to share my perception of clients' difficulties with male students, and enable them to formulate a model of work, particularly when the client was also male.

(Elsie)

Second, men students were seen as problematic in terms of their intervention with service users. For example, Linda described a man student who responded to women and men service users in the same way, whereas her expectation was that his responses would be differentiated according to the gender of the service user:

In looking at the strategies that he employed, it became clear that he utilised exactly the same strategy whether he was working with a male or female client, and initially could not identify any reason why that had produced very different outcomes. It was some time before he was able to identify that a root cause might be the gender considerations. My own frustration at him not being able to see this further impacted on the process, and we needed to take time out to explore his perceptions of me. At this time he stated that he perceived me as an aggressive female.

(Linda)

Third, the women social workers had experienced a reluctance by men students to engage with the impact of sexism:

I've had two male students. The last one I found a bit difficult to deal with. I wanted to start by talking with him about sexism in general and how he might be wording things differently to me or to a female client, and no matter what I said, it didn't really seem to strike a chord with him in the way I'd hoped it would and sometimes he'd be a little bit uneasy when I began to talk about sexism. It was hard really. He didn't really want to look at these areas. I think he wanted to in principle, but not really in practice. He was a bit uneasy. So, I found it very hard to make progress in addressing this. I didn't want to make him feel bad or uncomfortable. I wanted to approach the subject in a positive way. I did really want him to understand that there was a difference between opportunities available to him and opportunities available to a woman, in principle.

(Gaye)

Fourth, women social workers pointed to men students' lack of comprehension of women's experiences:

It is difficult, because some men, some male students, they appear not to understand what it is to be a female, or how we feel, or where we're coming from. He could not see why I was saying certain things about this female or this is how I really want you to do it. I found that bit difficult. Everybody comes from a different stance. You have to pick up quite clearly what level you've got to work with.

(Zina)

Fifth, this led one woman social worker to see men students as needing support:

I think I come from a team, this is awful to say this, perhaps, but our experiences of male students aren't particularly good. I wouldn't say negative, but they generally don't score as high as female student practitioners. You know, what we say is that they always sort of think with their dick, really, sometimes. They, I mean we have male students who will say, 'well, I think this is a male perspective on this', and it goes down like a lead balloon really. So, not to say that males get a raw deal of it as such, but I think in some ways they have to prove themselves a little harder, and that's in the team. On a personal basis, I have, over the years this is now, this isn't recent stuff, I'm talking about ever since I've been a practice teacher, I have probably had to stick up more for a male student than I have for a female student.

(Helen)

We have seen that the majority of the women social workers saw no possibility for developing egalitarian relationships with women service users based on shared experience nor, for that matter, did they perceive their relationships with women students in that light. Whilst needing to be cautious about inferring too much from the exploration of women social workers' experiences as practice teachers, it might be indicative of the even greater difficulties they would have encountered in seeking egalitarian relationships with women service users. Given their greater social distance from, and the stronger power relationship they have with, women service users, we can cautiously conclude that it is difficult to visualise the women social workers being able to construct relationships with women service users that would be more egalitarian than their relationships with women social work students, but there may be unacknowledged dimensions of shared experience with women service users, which fall short of egalitarian relationships, in the same way that there are with women students. Thus, some of the women social workers who were sceptical about shared experience with women students as the basis for more egalitarian relationships nevertheless identified particular difficulties in working with men that might suggest that there is a different, but unacknowledged, basis to their work with women students, albeit not extending as far as egalitarian relationships. There was a sense that working with women students was different to working with men, even though most of the women social workers did not go as far as seeing shared gender as leading towards egalitarian relationships with women students.

Empowerment

In Chapter 2 we saw that the feminist social work literature has stressed that the goal of feminist practice is the empowerment of women service users. 'Empowerment' was used by most of the women social workers to describe their approach to working with women service users. For Candy (one of only two of the social workers who described herself as 'feminist' – see Chapter 6), 'empowerment' captured the essence of applying feminism to her work with women service users:

> In terms of being aware of issues around women and trying to empower women in their lives, that's how I would see myself as a feminist. To raise their self-esteem, to raise their confidence, to enable them to make decisions for themselves. To feel they are able to make the decisions. To not feel as though they have to submit to another person's opinion. That they can be assertive and articulate in their lives. That's how I would see people, people feeling differently about themselves, people feeling that they have power to do something about their own lives, and by working with them, you know, specific tasks maybe that they have to do.
>
> (Candy)

Although Candy came closest to the sentiments concerning the goal of empowerment in the feminist social work literature, she slipped into talking about an approach that might be used in a similar way with any service user. This is indicated by the way in which she began by referring to 'women' and moved on to talking about 'people'. In terms of how this approach to people, which includes women, played out, it consisted of being alongside the woman service user and working with her against those who are trying to prevent her having a voice. However, there was no recognition of the woman service user needing to be empowered in the power relationship vis-à-vis women social workers.

This shades into the majority view, which was of the woman social worker enabling service users, in general and regardless of their gender, to participate in aspects of the work taking place with them:

> Empowering services users to participate fully in events, in reviews, that sort of thing, is important to try and alleviate oppression. Can we empower or enable clients? Where are you going to get the most effective change?
>
> (Theresa)

The approach Theresa suggested had two important points. First, it is a view of empowerment as participation in social work processes. Second, it is a general principle of participation that is applied to women's participation in social work, as it is to other service users. In this approach of empowerment-as-participation, the category 'woman' is no more or less significant than other categories, such as age:

I like to look at age and empowerment in relation to the vulnerability of the older person and issues around empowerment like shared responsibility.

(Gita)

This all-embracing, fairly elastic concept of empowerment-as-participation allowed the women social workers to use the term even when a service user was in very restrictive circumstances, such as 'empowering' a young person who had absconded:

We planned to empower a person in a powerless situation and to expand their choice to a maximum in a situation where choices appear to be restricted.

(Gaye)

The application of a general and ungendered principle of empowerment to women service users was apparent as Hilary talked about discussing anti-oppressive practice with a student in relation to work with a single parent:

In every case with a student, we actually look at what the main issues are, why are they there for that particular person? Are they a single parent family? Is it any wonder single parents have these difficulties, these problems? They are already oppressed by society. We have to consider what we can do as an individual worker to try and alleviate this oppression. Do we actually empower clients? Do we enable clients to make changes? What can we do to get the most effective changes?

(Helen)

Another aspect of empowerment that was put forward was the way in which a woman service user's sense of having things in common with other women could validate her personal experiences. Elsie described using a book in groupwork with women with depression:

I don't think I've had a women who said she couldn't read it and who couldn't actually see something of herself in the book. It's so empowering when they see that somebody has written down the sorts of things they've been thinking and feeling. It validates it so much. It is very empowering.

(Elsie)

The implication was that recognition of having experiences in common with other women depathologises service users' involvement with mental health services, at least to some extent.

Thus, empowerment in relation to women service users was seen as a component in a wider commitment to participation by all service users and was a fairly elastic concept. Only two of the women social workers questioned the elasticity of the term 'empowerment':

Empowerment is a word that drives me crazy because students talk about it all the time, without saying what it means or how they did it. I think if you asked any of the social workers in these two teams, in the two children's teams here, what empowerment meant, they would see that as working with service users or asking the opinions of service users.

(Liza)

One of the women social workers related a discussion she had had with a student in supervision, after the student had said she was taking a feminist perspective in relation to a single woman carer and had given this as an example of feminism as empowering practice:

When we're talking about empowerment, we are actually talking about anti-discriminatory practice really, aren't we, so, you know, if you're looking at women-centred perspectives, looking at how they are working with a single parent who is living in poverty, inadequate housing and got six kids, and they're telling me they're taking a feminist perspective and they're doing this and doing that, and I'm saying, well, okay, what does that actually mean then, for that woman, the fact that you are actually taking on this perspective? What does this mean for this woman? And you said to me that this is the conversation that you've had with her, how do you think this has left her feeling? So it's actually trying to get them to almost put themselves in the position of the service user, and get an idea of how they might feel, and get them to think through, well, what is this theory about and does it really empower this person? Are you really trying to give this person some choices? And how are you trying to give this person back some control?

(Olive)

In addition, this quotation illustrates a view of empowerment as the woman social work student giving the woman service user 'some control' back over her life and in the process indicates where power lies in the relationship.

These examples, drawn from women social workers' experiences, suggest a view of empowerment as consisting of women service users participating in decisions in ways that validate their experiences. As such, empowerment appears to be a general principle which is applied, or in some cases fine-tuned, to work with women service users, with little consideration of the power present in state social work (see Chapter 3). That power is there by implication, but attracts little direct consideration. This suggests that the women social workers' understanding and use of 'empowerment' was part of the mainstream approach to state social work that developed across the 1990s (see Chapters 4 and 5), an approach most clearly reflected in the concept of partnership.

Partnership

The above interpretation seems to be borne out by the women social workers who referred to partnership in relation to empowerment:

> I've looked at ways of making the assessment a shared document, so again, that's around issues of partnership and shared responsibility.
>
> (Gita)

> I aim to maintain respect for service users and work towards client self-determination, working in partnership with young people and their carers.
>
> (Ruth)

> You design your own programme, in partnership with parents, looking at the needs of the young person, and we work with the Criminal Justice Act and the Children Act, so we're very conscious of the need to work in partnership with the young person.
>
> (Helen)

> I like care management. I actually find I can use it to the client's advantage, and I much prefer the idea that the client's rights to see what is written about them are enshrined and it is not an optional extra anymore. I do feel that they are more likely to be partners in the assessment process.
>
> (Angela)

Whilst empowerment, in the main, was discussed uncritically as a way of representing women social workers' stance towards working with service users, partnership attracted more critical reflections. For example, one woman social worker saw it as ignoring the extent to which state social work is embedded in the social divisions of the wider society:

> Much of the work within a statutory agency is based on the values, laws and judgements of white, middle-class Britain. In direct contradiction to this, the majority of the service users have neither the privileges or the experiences of that group of society.
>
> (Ruth)

Partnership was seen as problematic in relation to the statutory-based inter-ventions employed by social workers:

> I mean, there's this notion of partnership, and I know that we are all equal, but some are more equal than others. I mean partnership is quite often forced, for things like child care and child protection.
>
> (Iris)

I don't think we've still sorted out partnership with parents, you know. Social workers don't look at power relationships and you can't say to someone, 'we're going to do this aren't we', and that be a partnership, you know. I mean I argue with people now who when we talk about, you know, referrals to associations like alcohol and drug advisory, you know, we work in partnership with service users. We don't, you know. If we've got a young parent here who is using drugs or alcohol we send them there. They have no choice in that. If they wish to keep their children, they go. So the partnership process is 'do I do as they say, or do I lose my child?'

(Liza)

Whilst sharing information with service users was seen as an example of partnership of which the women social workers approved, this caused real difficulties with some service users, which they felt were not recognised by their employing Social Services Departments:

It's meant to be about partnership. Having said that, I like to be flexible in the way I use assessments. Like, you must share your community care assessment with the client, but then with clients with dementia, you can't share it with them, you can try and share it with them. Their concentration span is usually about half a minute. I may be discriminatory in saying this but I think in some ways it's a waste of time, as long as you've told them what's going on, you've explained it to them as best you can, the fact that, that whether they should actually read the report you've written, I don't think is relevant. If they've got relatives caring, I like them to read the report so that they are aware of what's going on. So, I wouldn't want to follow everything to the letter. I like to be able to tailor it.

(Gita)

Chapter 6 showed that the majority of the women social workers either had some degree of attachment to a feminist stance or saw themselves as influenced by feminist principles, even though their responses were marked by ambiguity and ambivalence. As we saw earlier in this chapter, this did not lead them to advocate egalitarian relationships. When discussing their work, women social workers overwhelmingly dismissed the possibility of egalitarian relationships with women service users. At first sight, having rejected egalitarian relationships, their support for empowerment is puzzling. However, the term 'empowerment' was used in a more limited sense than is the case in the feminist social work literature. In the main, the women social workers used 'empowerment' as a synonym for participation and its use evoked little critical reflection. Partnership was seen as an expression of empowerment, but was seen as more problematic. Perhaps this is because empowerment was seen as a principle devoid of specific practice content. It was a principle concerned with the conduct of the process of social work on the part of the individual woman social worker. Whilst partnership also focused on the process of social work, there were explicit expectations of the social work mechanisms through which partnership with service users would be pursued, for example assessments and case conferences, and there were concrete outcomes to be achieved through the use of those mechanisms, again in partnership with service users. When the aims of state social work were brought into the picture, and were being pursued by means of partnership through legislative, policy and organisational mechanisms established by the state, constraints began to break through into the experiences of the women social workers. Thus, dilemmas and constraints emerged when the women social workers discussed their experiences of working in specific settings.

Working in specific settings

So far in this chapter we have examined women social workers' experiences in relation to egalitarian relationships and empowerment. We saw in Chapter 1 that feminist perspectives have been employed to open up analysis of specific areas of practice and some of the responses of women social workers in Chapter 6 referred to drawing on feminist understandings of particular areas of social work. Seven of the women social workers in the study were based in community care settings and twelve in child care settings, with one person having a generic role because of the specialised nature of her job as an out-of-hours duty social worker. We now turn to consider the women social workers' experiences in these settings and how they saw work in their particular settings as addressing the interests of women.

When the seven women social workers working in community care settings referred to work that addressed the interests of women, they focused, in the main, on informal carers with, in addition, one woman social worker raising assessment work and two commenting on women's experiences in relation to using mental health services.

One of the women social workers regarded some informal carers as having a psychological need to remain in the caring role:

> Well there will always be a fair number of cases where you've got women looking after people, who maybe haven't chosen that, but it's happened to them, and they've got a pattern of looking after one person. Then they die or whatever and then they latch onto another person. They don't know how to rebuild their life without being in a caring role.
>
> (Amy)

In contrast, the others thought that it was important to counter the assumption that women would be the informal carers:

> When you're working with carers, well, you know, the majority of carers are female. Obviously as a team I think we try, and as individual workers, we

try not to make sort of assumptions about the gender of carers, try not to assume that women should be the carers.

(Candy)

Gita thought that countering this assumption involved confronting men, when this became necessary:

Perhaps in society more than in social services there's this feeling that if a husband is going back to his wife, there's less questioning about whether she can cope than if it was a wife going back to her husband. Perhaps, not through prejudice, but through knowing that in the majority of households the wife has traditionally done all the work, so you do need to ask if the husbands can do it, are prepared to do it, and that sort of thing.

[Q: What if men say they are not prepared to do it?]

You've got to take care of your client, so you can go out and read the riot act. It's very difficult. I think I'd put a carer in, a female carer, if he wasn't prepared to do it after that, because you can't force anybody to do anything. You've got to look for ways round it. Someone standing their ground categorically, saying they're not going to do anything, I've never had that situation.

(Gita)

Gita's response fitted with Orme's view that

Gender as a dimension is often lost or denied when the focus is on the predominant characteristic of the group as identified by the administrative categories of community care provision. More significantly, attention to gender, if it does occur, often involves treating men and women differently. In doing so, men and women who are in receipt of community care are frozen into fixed identities which are prescribed by stereotypical assumptions about masculinity and femininity.

(Orme 2001: 215–216)

Theresa emphasised the need to avoid falling into negative portrayals of carers, when discussing the work of a student on placement with her:

Caring situations pose a clear issue around gender expectations. Quite recently we had a case, an older woman, who had moved to this area, moved only because, after her husband died, the family felt that she would be better off moving to this area, to be closer to them. It seemed reasonable but I think maybe they hadn't explored how she felt about it very much, so when she came up here, she seemed to fall into some sort of depression, wasn't well motivated to do all the things that she used to do, and the student's involvement at that stage was a response from the carer to say what can we actually do to help my mother? Because she doesn't seem to be functioning very well, and she's got arthritis, she's not getting out very much and the issue for the carer at that time was the ill-health of the older person. What can you do about it? She needs day care, needs this, that and the other. Quite clearly, as the student started to learn, the issues were more complex than that. It was about loss, loss of partner, loss of identity because she had moved from an area to somewhere completely new. She wasn't seeing as much of the family as they had led her to believe she would, so there were all those kinds of issues that needed to be looked at. But then, from the carer's perspective, seeing the decline in her mother's health was putting pressure on her, on the carer, and when we first became involved, the student's response was, what an unpleasant woman this carer is because she was making all these demands on us, you know, when she should be doing them, sort of thing. So obviously to me there was a big issue there about gender expectations, which we had to unravel and it got quite tense between this student and myself, trying to unravel that. Because what I sensed was, I wouldn't call it an intuitive response, but a hasty response, a judgement that was made, that to me indicated a value base that needed sorting out. So we had to do quite a lot of work on that and I suppose for me, one of the first indications, a bit of a concern about value base expectations, making assumptions, that needed sorting out. So that, it obviously was a gender issue.

(Theresa)

Only one woman social worker talked specifically about women service users' interests, as against carers' interests, as part of the assessment process:

I think if you were assessing a couple, for example, then you would look at any gender issues between that couple and assessing the woman as being oppressed and therefore your work would be sort of, try and sort of re-adjust that balance, to empower that woman within that relationship. So I think issues of gender come into that.

(Candy)

Two women social workers discussed the high referral rates of women to mental health services, which they considered were a reflection of women's position in society:

Well, there is a great deal of poor female mental health which is directly attributable to women's position in society and their specific individual position in the culture, the family, that they live in and that is so, it is sort of endemic, and it doesn't, it's worse if you live in the lower classes because of the poor housing, because of the poverty, because life is that much harder, but interestingly, it's still there in quite upper middle classes, where they've got more choices because they've got more money and they've had more education, but still you quite often find women are there and sometimes maybe even because the husband or whatever is in business and therefore he's been you know, quite ruthless and you know, getting up the ambition ladder and all the rest of it, and he tends to be very oppressive towards his wife, in spite of the fact that they've both had more education and opportunity because they're better off.

(Elsie)

Gaye expressed concern about women being compulsorily admitted to psychiatric hospitals, particularly black women:

I have to attend to people at the police stations, so, I've very often talked about the position of women who are detained at the police stations under the Mental Health Act. I always talk about the possibility and usually the presence of sexist attitudes by the police. I thought, we could look at ethnic monitoring on assessments and that led into looking at the authority-wide monitoring which showed that women are more likely to be sectioned and that black women are more likely to be sectioned as well, basically.

(Gaye)

The women social workers who were located in child care settings considered that they were addressing women's interests simply because the majority of services users with whom they worked were women:

I think gender seems to run as a common vein throughout all the work, if you look at it. I mean, if you look at the number of, I mean we will look at in supervision with students, you could look at the number of women. Look at duty for example, in a typical week or in a typical day, who has the most interaction? You will find it will be a female.

(Hilary)

Ninety-nine per cent of social work, it is with the mothers who come, which I think is very oppressive and it is very hard to break that because fathers, some quite often come to first interviews, but then leave it to mum because he's working. So we do a lot of discussion around how we can work against that and how we try not to create situations which are as oppressive as whatever is going on outside which is causing the problem in the first place.

(Janis)

Again, in child protection work, the bulk of it is with females. It is actually done with females.

(Liza)

Having identified that the majority of the service users were women, and concluded, ipso facto, that their work addressed women's interests,[2] a significant dimension that was seen as impacting on women's interests was the contribution, or lack of it, to child care by men. This is mirrored in the practice of social workers, which often does not engage with men. A number of writers have highlighted the exclusion of men from child care issues, particularly in relation to work aimed at child protection (Milner 1993, 1996; Corby 1993; O'Hagan and Dillenburger 1995; Edwards 1998). Drawing on the work of Milner, Christie found that

> fathers were systematically excluded from the child protection system, with social workers often taking the place of absent fathers and primarily monitoring women's ability to care for their children. The ambiguous nature of fatherhood results in social workers having unclear expectations about the roles of fathers in caring for children.
>
> (Christie 2001: 30)

These low expectations lead to men being both absent and absented from contact with social workers (Edwards 1998: 266), a tendency identified by the women social workers:

> I like to think that I'm reasonably vigilant about issues around making sure that fathers are seen as equally responsible and that as far as possible social workers make the effort to connect with the fathers as well as the mothers in the families and don't collude with sexist ideas and expectations. I am sure this is not as rigorous as it should be.
>
> (Anita)

> You know, the majority of single families are female families, and yet we would draw a distinction within supervision when we would actually have the odd referral of the male single parent family and we treat them differently. Do we treat them differently? You know, I think we do. Like, for example, child minding. If a female carer wants to go out to work, then it's her responsibility to arrange her child care arrangements. Yet if a male walks through our door, it's almost like, they won't be able to function properly with children, and so, there's more onus I feel in the use of Section 17 to provide that support. So I think we do stereotype, we run into those pitfalls really, time and time again.
>
> (Hilary)

The pitfalls of stereotyping were also highlighted in relation to expectations about women caring:

> A lot of the difficulties this particular client faces are to do with poverty and being a woman in a society which expects women to care, but provides no support. Women's identity and self-esteem is tied up with her own and others' perspectives of how caring she is as a woman.
>
> (Anita)

I was dealing with a case where the mother had left her four children with her partner, who was having difficulty coping. It was very easy for me as a worker assessing the possibility of the children being rehabilitated to the mother, when she eventually requested it, to focus on her not having fulfilled her maternal role. A colleague within the team, who was doing a course in women's studies, was able to highlight for me the tendency to feed into gender stereotypes. It seemed to me then that society was more tolerant of men abdicating their parenting responsibilities. One could say that it was not a deliberate or a conscious oppressive practice, but it made me aware of the potential for female workers to be sexist.

(Donna)

Another area related to women and their role as carers was fostering. Cindy's view was that although she would not agree that women should automatically take on this role, it was hard to work against organisational policies and practices:

I think the whole thinking, the whole issue within fostering, there are so many things that are, you know, originally it was seen as a female, something that females would do and the way, how do we make sure that we don't discriminate, and I guess make assumptions about women within a fostering role, it's quite important, and the way that we can access more males, getting them more involved in caring, so I think it does come up. I hate to say that perhaps it's a lower priority within the department at the moment, just because of time, and how do we, how do we get more male carers on board?

(Cindy)

In the field of youth justice, Helen thought that how women young offenders were viewed by the courts was problematic:

There's a lot of gender issues, for instance, how people are treated in court, and sometimes, you get a problem where the magistrates view a young woman in a certain way because of her lifestyle, which wouldn't happen with a young man, and it can work either way for them and sometimes, it sounds awful again, but if they go in a short skirt and they are very attractive and they flutter their eyelashes at the male magistrates they can get a better sentence. You know, appearances are really important in court. It sounds dreadful, but it's true.

(Helen)

In both community care and child care settings the women social workers focused overwhelmingly on women as carers in discussing the points at which women service users' interests were addressed in their practice, rather than, for example, also highlighting to the same extent how the interests of women with disabilities, older women, girls and young women might be addressed. Although women social workers saw themselves as addressing the interests of women in the context of their caring roles, they were also conscious of the potential for reinforcing the stereotypical roles assigned to women as carers through social work. Dominelli takes this point further, by suggesting that

> Though critical of women's best efforts and aware of the commonalities which bind them across the gender divide, women social workers, no less than their male counterparts, expect women to manage in the most obdurate social conditions and berate them when they fail.
>
> (Dominelli 2002b: 2)

Conclusion

In the sense conveyed by the feminist social work literature, we have seen little evidence in this chapter of the existence of egalitarian relationships between women social workers and women service users. There did appear to be a level of unacknowledged shared experience, which falls short of the possibility of egalitarian relationships, but there was also a tendency for women social workers to refer to women service users as 'females'. Given that 'female' is not used very much by women as a synonym for 'woman' in everyday life, it may indicate the sense of distance that these women social workers experienced in relation to women service users, as a result of their position in state social work. This may also explain why a certain amount of shared experience with women, as implied by difficulties experienced with men, seemed to go unacknowledged.

In contrast, there was strong support for 'empowerment' from the women social workers, used in a loose way to refer to encouraging service users' participation in social work. The support for empowerment may have been sustained by its malleability in terms of support for an abstract principle. This seems to have been suggested by the contrast between how 'empowerment' and 'partnership' were seen. Although seen as an expression of empowerment, partnership was regarded as problematic. Perhaps the explicit expectations and anticipated outcomes of the latter led women social workers away from abstract principle and back into the dilemmas and constraints of state social work, some of which emerged when the women social workers discussed their experiences of working in specific settings.

Having considered feminist identity in the previous chapter and egalitarian relationships and empowerment in this chapter, Chapter 8 moves on to examine women social workers' experiences of the impact of managerialism on their practice, and the tensions involved in occupying managerial positions.

Managerialism and practice

After discussing the defining characteristics of state social work in Chapter 3, Chapter 4 charted the development of managerialism in Social Services Departments. This managerialised context represents the field of possibilities within which women's interests have to be addressed in state social work and so the present chapter examines the women social workers' experiences of key aspects of these managerial developments and their responses to them.

Positive experiences of managerialism

Eleven of the women social workers spoke favourably about aspects of tighter managerial control over practice that they had experienced. Those from community care settings thought that the system that had been introduced following the NHS and Community Care Act 1990 had encouraged and enabled social workers to include service users in assessment and report-writing processes. This was seen as having reinforced good social work practice, defined by what they saw as empowerment (see Chapter 7). They regarded the participation of service users as an important gain in the years following the implementation of the Act, which they saw as having encouraged more openness and accountability:

> I like care management, and although a lot of people say, 'well, we find our hands tied, it's so reductionist, it's so this, it's so that', I actually find that I can use it to clients' advantage, and I much prefer the idea that the client's rights to see what's written about them are enshrined and it's not an optional extra anymore, that I do feel that they are more likely to be partners in the assessment process.
>
> (Angela)

The standardisation brought about by managerialism was seen as resulting in more equitable treatment of service users:

> There is some standardisation, but in some ways that isn't a bad thing, because everybody [service users] gets a fair crack at it I think. And so I'm pretty

optimistic and positive about care management. I feel if I was out there on a patch now,* I would still work the same as I did before. I would use the policies and procedures for my use, the clients' use. I don't think there's any need to see it as stifling.

(Amy, *team manager)

Clear procedures were seen as clarifying what had to be done in social work:

I actually came in [to social work] as a trainee child care officer. I did a year's training as a child care officer and then they implemented the Seebohm Report. I left to have my children at this point and when I came back we were expected to do older people and everything. I don't think I ever really got over that period. In child care, we had no procedures, it was incredibly hit-and-miss. I was taken out by a senior and helped to sort of snatch some children away from somebody once. It was awful, very oppressive. When I came back [into social work] and found that there were procedures, you know, when I had a suspected child abuse come in, and there was a manual with a list of things, a checklist of things you should know, it was so reassuring that there was something there that I could use, you know, to back me up. With regards to the older people, adults, that I now work with, I started pre-Community Care Act, quite early on, the access to records, that legislation came in so we had all this stuff on how to record things and the fact that people could go to see a file. I think that made you tighten up on your recording, made you think about what you were writing down. And I think that was anti-oppressive. I think it's good and it's right to have the guidelines that we have.

(Gita)

The women social workers who worked in child care settings, and who were positive about the changes which had taken place, approved of the Children Act 1989 and subsequent central and local government procedures and guidelines. Before the introduction of the Act, some aspects of practice were seen as haphazard:

It definitely changed the way we work. There are lots of things in the Children Act now we have to follow. Prior to the Children Act it was really haphazard practice I think. The Children Act provided clear guidance, a clear way of moving forward.

(Zina)

The reform of child care policy was seen as having moved social workers' practice in the direction of firmer boundaries and more accountability for their practice:

I certainly think there was a change for the better, with the Children Act. I think that it made a really big impact on how we actually work. When I look back at practices like Place of Safety Orders, I mean they were like two-a-penny. I could have done one blindfolded, and when you look at the practices, it really makes you sort of, you know, fall over really, because you could take a Place of Safety and a parent wouldn't see their child for 28 days. And really that's not on. So, we are much more accountable for our practice these days, you know. I mean orders, a removal of a child, must be the last recourse. So we're working within much firmer boundaries.

(Hilary)

Tighter timescales were seen as a positive development:

I mean, there was a mixed reaction I think from social workers, where some people felt like it was the best thing that ever happened, that they liked the clear guidelines and being told what they'd got to do and when they'd got to do it and being given very strict timings on things. I think time limits are fine.

(Liza)

The women social workers identified the positive features of managerialism as being clear procedures, which provided tighter boundaries for their work, involving a more standardised approach (and hence they argued a more equitable approach) to practice. They also welcomed the encouragement of service user participation and stressed the importance of social workers' accountability. Their welcome for these aspects of managerialism can be seen as a commitment to what they regard as good practice, together with an appreciation of greater predictability in their work because they know where they are and what they are supposed to do. Although they present managerialism and good practice as operating in tandem, presumably there is the potential for their being on a collision course at times. For example, a particular course of action might seem to make sense and might have the support of a service user, but might be precluded by the more standardised, managerial approach which they welcomed for the reasons already cited. Thus the trade-off might be that whilst there may be more protection for services users against the arbitrary exercise of social workers' discretion (see Chapter 3), there may also be less chance of an individually attuned response:

In a statutory context, no matter how strongly you feel about a particular aspect of your work, or how strong your value base is, at the end of the day you are working within this agency where you may find that your value bases have no use at all, because you are going to have to do something completely different. And that could be something as simple as a particular service provision, which you feel is desperately needed, but because of, I don't know, criteria or priorities, within the agency, you're not going to be able to provide it.

(Theresa)

Negative experiences of managerialism

The women social workers identified six aspects of the impact of managerialism on their work as negative: increased involvement in financial matters, shortage of resources, having to remain within 'core business', the closing down of practice possibilities, computerisation and loss of discretion. Each of these aspects is considered in turn.

Financial aspects

The women social workers who worked in community care settings did not like having to elicit financial details from service users for the purpose of means-testing their eligibility for services:

> I suppose we are having a lot more input into finances which we never used to have. A lot of social workers feel that it's an intrusion on people's privacy, that we shouldn't be expected to handle this.
>
> (Theresa)

Shortage of resources

The community care participants were also struggling with constraints imposed by limited resources, which they saw as undermining the stated policy goals which were meant to be achieved by the community care reforms:

> I think the real hang-up now is just about resources and, you know, anything outside of the resources forum is seen as almost irrelevant anymore. It just feels that, you know, you're so busy fighting for what you can actually get in respect of services.
>
> (Ruth)

This was seen as having resulted in the disappearance of the flexible approach to services, which was meant to be the hallmark of community care:

> What's stifling is that there's no money, so we can't actually give people a flexible care package to meet the needs that we've assessed.
>
> (Liza)

> When you're doing your assessments, there's a particular service that's needed and is just not available because there isn't any money, or whatever the reason is.
>
> (Amy)

Restrictions on particular resources were sometimes experienced as happening in an arbitrary manner:

I mean, when I was at ['X'] Road, they suddenly decided that the department would no longer supply bath aids to the majority of the population. Well, with older people that's one of the first things that they actually need, so when you were on duty you would get two or three times a day, somebody ringing up, I can't get into the bath, please can you help me get into the bath and you have to say, sorry, no. We can give you an assessment. If you've got one of these conditions then we can help you, you know, and all that, so you were restricted in that sense.

(Gita)

The pressure was perceived in terms of prioritising the need to divert older people from residential care, with other services suffering as a result:

Money is limited, certainly for young people with disabilities, trying to get the home adapted, that is a major financial hurdle, or financing respite for a lone parent, who is just struggling really, just needs some time to themselves, to be an adult for a couple of hours a week.

(Ruth)

For some of the participants, stretched material resources pointed to the need for social workers to draw on their internal resources:

I mean, I think we are, we are increasingly in a situation where you can get hung up on the fact that there aren't the resources to do things, and it would be very easy to curl up in a little ball and say, you know, well I can't do it, there's no money to do it. But I think it actually, it's really important that we don't actually allow that to happen and that we do find alternative ways of accessing resources and that may mean actually accessing resources within us.

(Linda)

Other participants thought that managerial processes simply threw into sharp relief what had been long-standing issues in social work:

It just seems as though it's become a more streamlined process now, the access to resources, so that when you can't get everything you want, it feels to the individual social worker that it's like the end of the world but it always used to be like that anyway. It's just the process that's different.

(Theresa)[1]

Core business

We saw in Chapter 4 that one of the ways in which managerialism has impacted on public sector organisations has been with regard to identifying their 'core business'. This involved setting clear primary goals and shedding activities that did not contribute to their achievement. The women social workers talked, unprompted, about 'core business' in their Social Services Departments and about what core business comprised. Managerial definitions of 'core business' clearly influenced the services that users received. Dominelli has argued that ideas about core business lead to the commodification of services, with their users being

> in danger of losing their dignity as people with a voice which is their own. Instead, they are obliged to frame their concerns within the tramlines established by policymakers, professional experts and entrepreneurs, whose ideas about which services are suitable dictate what become available.
>
> (Dominelli 2002c: 142)

Some participants went to great lengths to define the work that constituted core business in relation to their departments' priority levels. These accounts gave glimpses of how women social workers are involved day-to-day in calculating priorities, rejecting work and, in the process, controlling the allocation of resources:

> Well, we've had to tighten up. We used to cover three levels, priority 1, 2 and 3. Priority 1 is to do with needing support your whole life, activities, that sort of thing. Priority 2 is needing quite a lot of support. Priority 3 is needing a minimal amount, so, like, priority 3 would be a straightforward home care referral, or benefits, wanting benefits advice, possibly housing, that sort of thing. We're not supposed to get involved with priority 3s. So what we have to do is go back to the ward staff and tell them to either direct the referral to the local social services office for home care or to CAB for benefits. Now, we are also acting as liaison workers with particular wards, and so sometimes the staff on the ward would ask us general questions about a client they weren't quite sure about and it would perhaps help if we saw them and just sort of clarified things. But, at the moment, we've got so much work coming in that we're supposed to bring all the referrals back here and then ['X'] prioritises them, so we're a bit restricted. I'm very reluctant to go in to talk to anybody because you often start something off that you can't really finish. So I feel restricted in that sense, but you can't just say to the nurses, 'Oh, I'll have a word'. I find I'm saying to them, would you go and talk to them again and make sure whether it's going to be for us and if it's not for us then can you deflect it somewhere else.
>
> (Gita)

Despite the influence exercised by 'core business', it was not regarded as being set in stone and never negotiable. Some participants suggested that teams can develop norms which bend the commitment to core business on occasions:

> Well, you see here, I would say the manager is a core business manager but he also accepts that there are times when you need flexibility with a case, but

it's a question of just convincing him that the work is really required, and that's all it takes, because he's accepted that he's not going to prevent people from doing what they really think is social work. But I suppose it makes it easier if people just go along the core business route. It's easier to manage, isn't it? He is the sort of person who likes to keep a tight rein on everything, and he'd be the first to admit it. But you only need to approach him to get it sorted. So, maybe there is a team culture that would make it easier or more difficult to work round core business.

(Theresa)[2]

In addition to teams remoulding what counts as core business, the women social workers considered that once allocated to work with a service user the social worker still enjoyed a measure of discretion in how the work was carried out:

I think, you can obviously only work with people where the referral is sort of core business, where, you know, at the moment it's sort of fairly urgent referrals, but when you are actually given a piece of work, then you still have quite a lot of scope as to how you carry out that work, and I guess in those ways you can work towards empowering, you know, the family members, the service user themselves.

(Candy)

Such experiences of continuing discretion have been supported elsewhere (Evans and Harris 2004) but have not been countenanced in some of the feminist social work literature, with Dominelli, for example, maintaining that 'the commodification of clients' choices is paralleled by the commodification of professional labour. In the process, professional autonomy is effectively curtailed, and the practitioner's capacity to exercise professional discretion in responding to individual need is thereby limited' (Dominelli 2002c: 145).

If we refer back to Derber's work on ends and means (see Chapter 3), the women social workers' view of discretion seemed to be about the means of working with individual service users in terms of the social worker's discretion in the conduct of the relationship, hence the emphasis on 'empowerment' (and see Chapter 7). Discretion is discussed more fully on pages 123–125.

Closing down practice possibilities

Despite a degree of negotiability in some teams, as a result of managerial control being exerted over definitions of what constituted core business, working methods regarded in the feminist social work literature as compatible with feminist practice (see Chapter 2) were seen by the women social workers as having little prospect of being realised. Three forms of social work were mentioned as either having been marginalised or excluded from their work: collective work, preventive work and counselling.

Collective work

Dominelli has maintained that 'feminist social workers can affirm collective solidarities that have been unhelpfully dismissed and sacrificed to individualism' (Dominelli 2002b: 8). In contrast, the social workers in community care settings rejected the possibility of collective work with service users:

> I don't think it is realistic, although we'd like, you know, we'd love to. But I just can't see us getting the approval to do that sort of work. I mean students could. They don't have the same sort of pressure on them to do just core business. I haven't known many social workers do that sort of work.
>
> (Denise)

Whilst participants thought that there might be benefits in moving beyond individual responses to women who were experiencing similar difficulties or who were requesting similar forms of support from services, they were sceptical about the possibilities of formulating such responses:

> There is a carers' group, and it's, and we still have, there is still one social worker in the team who actually, she's in a joint role with a nurse, that's the way it's been going for years. I can't see us getting the funding or the, sort of, the agreement to actually run a new group. I mean, the only groups that I know that have been set up in the last few years have been those when the students have done them, but maybe in the voluntary sector you can. I can't see it in the present social work climate here. Although it used to be, it even just sort of, I mean, a few years ago it used to be something that was talked about in team meetings, but not any more.
>
> (Candy)

Although some of the women social workers considered that there were benefits to be gained in establishing various groups for women (for example, for carers, women with depression, single parents), they saw this as difficult to achieve and it remained only as a pipe dream in supervision sessions:

> I think, within your own supervision, it is easier to keep that alive and it's easy to talk about a woman's isolation in the community and how can we put something in there to support her as a woman in the community and help build her self-esteem. But, outside of supervision, the reality is very much that this will not happen.
>
> (Ruth)

One participant who was still working with groups of women was finding it increasingly difficult to do so:

> I've done groupwork packages for working with depressed women, where they are, I suppose if you want a more general description, sort of downtrodden

by society and their situation in life and being stuck at home with small kids. I've also had people with post-natal depression in that group. It's certainly getting harder to work with quite a large group of women who can benefit enormously. Their only point of contact, usually, is the GP who may be nice and listen and say, 'well never mind, dear, come back again next week and tell me how you're getting on', or he may just tell her to pull herself together like a pair of curtains, and it's getting harder to work with those women because of the government's push that we should be working with the severely mentally ill, you know, mad axe-men and all that. So that is a restraint which is getting ever greater.

(Elsie)

For those who tried to establish groups, difficulties arose over funding, because this aspect of work was not seen as core business:

Our service manager is very keen on anti-racist and anti-sexist practice and she supports me quite a lot and she would actually try to find some money, if I wanted to run a group, but because the department doesn't seem to be that committed to it, it's very difficult to get any time or money set aside to do the work we need to do.

(Helen)

A team manager thought it was unfair to see the demise of groupwork as a consequence of the impact of managerialism on social work:

There weren't very many groups before community care when I came here. They don't do any groupwork here now and this team is nothing like under pressure the way the others are. I think some people find it's useful to say, 'well, I can't do it anymore' because they probably didn't want to do it in the first place.

(Amy)

The ambivalence of Amy's response was revealed as she went on to explain that although, in principle, she would be happy to allow staff to participate in group-work she regarded this as problematic for reasons that related to her view of core business:

You can't spare people to go and do groupwork, because it's not crisis work. In principle, I'm happy for people to do groups, but it's got to be something that's worthwhile, not something I fancy doing so I can go off for several hours and I'm planning my groups, so everyone else is running, you know, doing the day-to-day work while you're off supposedly planning, and there's very little evidence, you know, it's hard to actually get evidence that someone is actually using their time properly. Our first duty under the Community Care

Act is to assess, and we've got timescales, so if people are off doing
groupwork, then they can't do their assessments and we're not meeting our
legal obligations and our departmental, well our declaration to the public, that
we will do this within so many weeks, days, or whatever, and we publish
that in the Community Care Plan. I can't see any reason why people shouldn't
do some groupwork, but my feeling is that people would not want to do it as
well as their casework. They would want to leave the casework, jettison quite
a lot. My problem would be to think about the rest of the team who would
have to possibly carry the extra load.

(Amy)

Preventive work

The women social workers described the work they did as 'high risk' or 'high
profile' and references were made to losing the 'nicey bits' and 'the little fillers'
they associated with preventive work:

I mean, preventive work is minimal, these days. That just always seems to lose
out. I mean, we are basically high profile, basically first base for, you know,
client interaction and stuff, and you know, it's high risk stuff that we
deal with. So all the other nicey bits that would average out your case load
are no longer there. These days all we ever have is either high risk or child
protection stuff. It's really hot stuff.

(Hilary)

The loss of the 'little fillers' had made the job less cheerful:

We're only picking up things that are fairly heavy, that need a lot of input, and
you don't get the little fillers, which, like, you know, made your day a bit more
cheerful. You could talk to somebody for five minutes and solve all their
problems, you know. You don't get that, so it's restricting in that sense.

(Gita)

Preventive work was seen as having largely disappeared:

Well, since I've been here, it's never been preventive. It's always been very
heavy-ended stuff. It feels like we're doing more and more of the child
protection. Before it was accommodation and stuff. I suppose for experienced
staff, all you seem to get is assessments, child protection and there is no
creativity.

(Iris)

I mean, we're very limited to what we can actually support, and in, sort of,
preventive areas of work we do very little because we just haven't got the

bodies to deal with it, so we tend to deal with stuff that's escalating and might not have reached child protection, but would be quite serious children in need, and you're immediately in there with a sticking plaster, and you're not really addressing the root problems of what might be the issues for the family. In fact I often think, you don't ever really get to know what they are, unless for some reason a case becomes a long-term involvement.

(Ruth)

Counselling

The women social workers raised the subject of counselling within their work. Their views were divided between those who saw counselling as possible, not-withstanding the constraints imposed by 'core business', and others who saw counselling as only possible outside statutory settings. Thus some of them thought that although work might be prioritised by managerial systems, once allocated, counselling was still possible with women service users:

> The service that we can't provide now, that we used to be able to, like the counselling bit, it doesn't figure much in social work, you could do that, quite legitimately, because there is a fear as well, and people have said it here, even within the team, team members, that, 'oh we can't do things like that', but you can, if you can argue a good enough case, then you will be allowed to do it. It's just that, I suppose, because of the pressure of work, it seems easier to close it off anyway.
>
> (Theresa)

Some stressed the importance of incorporating counselling within assessment work:

> I think there is still time and space for using counselling skills in the assess-ment interview and in the follow-up work and the social worker should be doing that. I think that some of them are doing that, but they maybe don't recognise it because they think, unless I do a counselling session, or I set a group up and do a group with someone, that's not real social work. It's actually underselling their activity.
>
> (Amy)

> We still have scope as to how we carry out our work, as long as we're not spending huge amounts of time, I mean on things like counselling. It's not considered core business in itself, although it could be part of an assessment.
>
> (Candy)

Others thought service users would only be able to receive counselling outside statutory settings:

We wouldn't be encouraged to adopt what's called counselling when there are skilled counsellors that can do that in other organisations. But you can have a counselling approach, and maybe prolong the case for a number of weeks because it's needed. But most social workers will shy off that, because it is not part of their work.

(Theresa)

We deal with child protection and then whatever comes to light. If the client needed counselling we would buy the service and that's why I'm probably de-skilled. I did a counselling course at ['X'] university. I got a Diploma in Counselling. I don't use it.

(Zina)

As far as these women social workers were concerned, only very limited opportunities, in only some settings, remained for collective work, preventive work or counselling within state social work. Such forms of practice were seen as having been curtailed by the introduction of managerialism, manifested in the concept of 'core business'.

Computerisation

As we saw in Chapter 4, a significant managerial development in recent years has been the increased use of information technology systems in Social Services Departments. The Social Services Departments where the women social workers were employed used computerised records of assessments and continuing work. The women social workers took this for granted as part and parcel of their working life:

Social workers must spend probably half their working hours sitting in front of a computer screen. That ain't social work, as most people think of it, but that is the reality.

(Elsie)

Theresa had found computerised record-keeping limiting:

I think it's just become more bureaucratic. I mean a lot of people [social workers] are getting to like it now. They use it a lot more than me. I have management functions on it, but I don't have the day-to-day functions, although I am aware of how to do it. I don't do as much as the practitioners. There are aspects of computerisation that have been absolutely painful to come to terms with. The drawbacks to me are the details that you can't put on. It's very limited.

(Theresa)

Elsie outlined some of what she saw as the negative aspects of computerisation for her work as a practitioner in the mental health field. First, she saw the decision to have all assessments and service users' records computerised as a means of managers overseeing more closely the workload of social workers. The data the computer system produced provided them with statistical information on resources and finances:

> I mean, as a statistical base, you know, I've got this many clients I'm working with, fine, but that's not what it's for. It's meant to replace all our recording. It's very much for financial control, very much. The way the programme has been designed, as far as I can see, is like, you know, a business. Somebody is ordering something so you order it from the production department and it costs this much, you know, and then it gets sent out, and then it's finished with and the order is complete, and it's very much based on that kind of thing. But if you are trying to put a service package together, we've got to use it because if we want money for somebody for something, you can't get the money unless all the information is on the computer, so those people, there are very few people actually, that we do get money for, but where that happens it will have to go on as a service package.
>
> (Elsie)

Elsie's view of computerisation as primarily providing a means of surveillance and control by managers (see Chapter 4) was reflected in her frustration concerning the lack of utility the system had in relation to her practice in a mental health setting:

> I went on a mental health [computer] users' group when we first did the course training, and we argued for some decent pick-lists[3] of the kinds of problems that people have and the type of work we do with them. We were saying, we want some proper things on there or else we're not doing it.
>
> (Elsie)

Although none of the women social workers identified any potential in developments connected with information technology, Dominelli anticipates that

> an important dimension for future deliberation and action is using computer-based technologies to assist social workers in undertaking their tasks in ways that are consistent with feminist principles. Access to these technologies and questions about who controls them remain crucial topics for further discussion.
>
> (Dominelli 2002b: 164)

A theme running through the aspects of the impact of managerialism considered so far has been the women social workers' experiences of discretion. The next section examines this in more detail.

Loss of discretion

The in-roads made by managerialism into social workers' use of discretion were discussed in general terms in Chapter 4. The women social workers discussed their experiences in relation to the exercise of discretion:

> I mean, the changes have been phenomenal, as you can imagine, from social work in the 1970s, when there was no accountability at all, and team leaders, they wouldn't be called managers for heaven's sake, wouldn't even dare say to us, 'Where are you going? What time could we expect you back here?' They wouldn't dare to say that because you were autonomous. And now we've gone from that to clocking in and clocking out and being very accountable.
>
> (Angela)

As we have seen, women social workers appreciated the boundaries established by the Children Act 1989 and the NHS and Community Care Act 1990 and by national and local policy guidelines because they valued the 'good practice' aspects of those boundaries and because they knew where they were. Thus, whilst recognising that the expression of legislation and policy in definitions of 'core business' meant they had little or no control over, in Derber's terms (see Chapter 3), the 'ends of their work', some women social workers considered they still had some autonomy about the 'means' by which those ends were achieved:

> I have more autonomy with my work at the health centre than I do here. But, even so, as long as we're working with core business here, then we still have, we do still have some scope as to how we carry out that work.
>
> (Candy)

Gaye contrasted the degree of autonomy she experienced as an out-of-hours duty social worker with that in a daytime team:

> I don't know, really know what all the constraints are, the checks and balances there are in an area team, although I get a flavour of it, and I'm quite glad I work from here [home]. My job is a bit unusual really, because it does leave a lot of free time, that I can go to other meetings, and work in groups at work, in a way where I'm not constrained by the checks and balances of the team.
>
> (Gaye)

In a health setting, a similar experience prevailed:

> A statutory setting has a lot of rules and regulations which they have to stick with which make them operate sometimes in a way which may be oppressive. We don't do that here. We work quite a lot with the health authority you see.

Ultimately the doctors carry the can, and we work in a way that seems appropriate with that particular person and it can be any way you choose really.

(Janis)

For some of the women social workers, the degree of autonomy they experienced was influenced by the team manager or the team manager's location:

To a great extent, I've got a lot of autonomy here, because there's no manager here. My manager is up the road. They know that we don't just do the people who social services say, you know, the priority levels criteria for services. If we did, we'd hardly see any. We'd only see people with psychotic illness, people who'd been in hospital, people who'd tried to kill themselves, which is quite different from when I first came to work here. And it's been brought about by government legislation, it's been brought about by rate-capping, as it used to be, ever-tightening. There is no money for this, this and this, but having said that, because we've got quite a lot of autonomy down here, there is a broader spectrum of people still seen. But that autonomy's going. It's going, slowly but surely it's going. Now my manager up the road is perfectly well aware that I'm seeing a slightly broader category of people than I should be, but they think that's a good idea you see, so they're not saying much about it, or else somebody above them will say, 'well, stop her from doing that'. So at a local level there is this sort of unspoken, 'yeah, well, we won't say too much about that'.

(Elsie, in a community mental health team)

Well, we're really lucky in this team. We have been like a hybrid from the start and we could buy in work if we wanted to buy in. We didn't actually pay for it, but you know what I mean. We could commission work from other teams or we could do it ourselves and we had a fairly forward-thinking manager so, although we have to work to national standards, the way we work isn't prescriptive, so you don't sort of get a young person that's done this so you pull out this programme and, you know, go through it automatically. You design your own programme, in partnership with parents, looking at the needs of the young person.

(Helen, in a youth justice team)

The women social workers' accounts of their experiences suggested that there were greater degrees of autonomy and discretion in out-posted jobs (Candy at a health centre, Gaye with the out-of-hours team and Janis in the health service team) and/or in settings that had a multi-disciplinary component (Candy and Janis again, and also Helen in youth justice). This suggests that the interaction of different managerial regimes in such settings makes it more difficult for managerial initiatives emanating from within Social Services Departments to operate to the extent that they do in settings which are clearly located within a Social Services

Department. In relation to the latter settings, the women social workers' experiences suggest that negotiations with team managers may, if only at the margins, still allow women social workers some autonomy within which to exercise discretion and flexibility, but this remains at the level of work with individual service users. All of this suggests that the prospects for the forms of social work endorsed by the feminist social work literature were poor. Only one participant linked the discussion of discretion to feminism:

> When I first qualified, all the 'isms' were at the front of my mind. I do think we worked in a different environment then to where we are now, and I certainly feel, if I look back, it seemed, when I was a social worker then, there were more discussions around feminism and we were on strike, issues were important, and now, I guess that the climate has changed. I think we haven't got as much autonomy and that you're constrained more by policy and practices.
>
> (Cindy)

Conclusion

In this chapter women social workers identified the features of state social work organisations that impact on their practice. They explored positive and negative aspects of managerialism in their work contexts. The aspects of managerialism that were seen as positive were the 'good practice' associated with consistency of decision-making and the encouragement of service user participation, together with an appreciation of greater predictability in their work. Other aspects of managerialism had negative connotations: increased involvement in financial matters; shortage of resources; pressure to remain within 'core business'; the closing down of practice possibilities (with regard to collective work, preventive work and counselling); computerisation; and loss of discretion. What these findings suggest, as anticipated in Chapter 2, is that the managerialism of state social work organisations was experienced by women social workers as antipathetic to proposals contained within the dominant paradigm of the feminist social work literature. How the women social workers accommodated to these negative features and the opportunities they identified to challenge managerialism are explored in the next chapter.

Chapter 9

Accommodations and challenges to managerialism

The managerialism of state social work organisations was experienced negatively in the main by women social workers and as running counter to the proposals for developing practice in the interests of women, contained in the feminist social work literature. The women social workers had to accommodate to these negative features in their day-to-day work and identified limited opportunities to challenge them within their employing departments, in relation to other statutory organisations, through the contribution of voluntary organisations and by linking with feminist activities on a wider front. These aspects of the women's working lives are explored before turning to the experiences of those who were already managers and the thoughts of others about moving into management.

Accommodations

Whatever the women social workers' views on managerialism (see Chapter 8), in their day-to-day work they had to reach accommodations with it. Elsie had worked out where the limits of her autonomy were and saw herself as working within them rather than having to negotiate the extent of her discretion on a day-to-day basis:

> I've been here so long I'm aware of how far I can go without running against a brick wall.
>
> (Elsie)

Linda, a manager, had a questioning approach to the procedures and guidelines within which she was expected to work:

> I still really live by the tenet that rules are there to help but are also there to be broken and so I see procedures and guidelines as a way of enabling us to work but not necessarily as being the way we should always work and so I see them as being something that is, if you like, it's, it's the framework, but that doesn't stop you putting different material on the inside. It doesn't stop you putting different pictures in. It doesn't stop you challenging. When I look back through my social work career, I mean, things that were policies and

procedures at the point when I started, are real no-nos now. Now if someone hadn't challenged them they'd still be the policies and procedures of today.

(Linda)

A similar approach was suggested by Cindy, a practitioner:

We can't change all the policies and procedures as perhaps we'd like to, but we can endeavour to put the needs of families and children first and ensure that, I guess, on a case-by-case basis that we're working as far as possible in an anti-discriminatory way.

(Cindy)

Janis stressed that state social work had always been shaped by legislation, which she regarded as a framework within which she sought to identify, and work within, the boundaries of her autonomy:

You've got to keep the standards up and I just think it's important that we do that. I've always tried to maintain a level of professionalism. It's about maintaining ground rules, being aware of what is your responsibility, what isn't your responsibility, what you can influence, what you can't influence. It's all very important. Social work has always been a method of social control, and whatever my principles, I have had to conform to the legislative framework of the day.

(Janis)

Challenges

The women social workers identified opportunities for challenging managerialism: within the Social Services Departments in which they were employed, in other organisational work settings, through links with voluntary organisations, as well as with feminist organisations and campaigns.

Within the employing department

The feminist social work literature (see Chapter 2) promotes the organisational context as an arena in which the existing priorities and orientation of services should be overhauled in the interests of women: 'feminist praxis . . . seeks to challenge and transform policy, practice and the organisation of service delivery, which constrains people in gender-specific roles or oppresses them by the inappropriate exercise of power' (Orme 1998: 227). The women social workers were pessimistic about being able to exert such influence. More generally, Jones has argued that

Professionals have become marginalised, partly as a result of managerialism, but partly because of their own inability to resist becoming agents of the state.

They have accepted social policy changes passively and, as a result, are now acting against rather than on behalf of their clients' interests.

(quoted in Harlow and Lawlor 2000: 51)

Angela's experience seemed to reflect this:

> I feel a bit defeated most days, both in terms of promoting myself as a lesbian and as a feminist, and trying to influence departmental perspectives about anti-oppressive practice. As Martina Navratilova said, if you want to know the difference between commitment and involvement, think of ham and eggs. The chicken is involved but the pig is committed and I start off being like the chicken, but by the end of the week I feel more like the pig. You just have to conserve your energy and pick fights that are most important.
>
> (Angela)

Some of the women social workers made a distinction between the team level and beyond that level:

> It's very, very frustrating. In terms of my immediate management and my team, it's very comfortable to challenge and to discuss and to try and move things on. So on a micro level I can do that. On a macro departmental level, it's much harder and the only way you can bring about change is to move things up the line management. We have a team briefing where it comes back from the director down and we're supposed to feed comments up, but I'm not sure how far up they go.
>
> (Iris)

The team level emerged as possessing possibilities for some variation in approach:

> We've probably got more time to think about anti-oppressive practice here than in [X] team. I think we have a chance to take issues up. It's a personal responsibility. It's to do with your environment, the support that is there. At [X], they had policies about oppressive language, etc., but in actual practice, I think it was very difficult.
>
> (Donna)

For many of the women social workers, the difficulties involved in challenging the use of oppressive language in the organisational context illustrated the obstacles in the path of change. Gaye said that she felt it was easier to confront services users about their language usage:

> I suppose, if I'm honest, more often than not, there are pressures against making challenges within the organisation. I find it easier when I'm working with children or teenagers or other service users.
>
> (Gaye)

In this sense, the focus for challenging oppression can easily become reduced to confronting language use by service users, rather than taking on powerful actors in the employing organisation. McLaughlin has suggested that this is learned when social workers are in training, with social work students being 'more likely to correct service users' language or attitudes than to challenge wider issues' (McLaughlin 2005: 299).

In contrast to Gaye, Linda, a manager, thought that careful use of terminology was a way of bringing about organisational changes in attitudes to women:

> I do place importance on terminology. It is not about getting into Personchester instead of Manchester, but actually making sure that staff talk about staffing a building and not manning a building. That we talk about increasing the number of staff hours, not man hours. I think if we can actually move away from gender-specific terminology as much as possible, without getting silly about it, then we can actually bring about a change in attitude because I do think language is very powerful in terms of changing attitudes.
>
> (Linda)

In general, practitioners were pessimistic about the impact they had, particularly when other women were using language that the women social workers regarded as oppressive:

> I think that the language that we use on the team is very, very masculinist. We use the word 'he' as a generic term for men and women, which I find offensive. When posters are put up like that, I ask for them to be taken down. Like, one went up a few weeks ago about 'Who is the client? He is the most important person who can walk through these doors. He is this, he is that'. I asked for that to be taken down and it was. That would have been a good opportunity for discussions about how a woman client coming through the door might have been made to feel invisible by that poster, let alone me as a woman worker. That's one example.
>
> (Anita)

> My suggestions for changing the language of the organisation are met with, 'oh well, she would say that wouldn't she, she's a man-hater'. So, if I suggest that we don't talk about manning the phones, or keeping master copies of things, I find I'm quite easily dismissed, because they think of me as quite an extremist. I can't claim to have made an impact at all.
>
> (Angela)

> Language doesn't change much. The hardest thing for me is the women who use the same language as the men and support the men when they are being sexist.
>
> (Denise)

In other organisational work settings

The feminist social work literature (see Chapter 2) has proposed that women social workers should not only regard their own organisations as a target for intervention in the interests of women but also should attempt to influence other agencies with which they come into contact. In relation to mental health services, for example, Barnes and Maple have argued that workers can develop practice by increasing their influence in organisations, through claiming more responsibility themselves on the basis of the knowledge and information they hold and through making alliances with others (Barnes and Maple 1992: 146). The three examples that follow draw on women social workers' experiences of working with other organisations; the first practitioner was from a youth justice team and the other two worked in a hospital social work department:

> You can feel oppressed as a professional in the police station and in the courts and the whole set-up in the police station is about oppression, isn't it really, and when you're a woman worker in the court you can feel very out of place because it's predominantly male and judges and magistrates can be judgmental and sexist.
>
> (Helen)

Gita and Angela had similar concerns about working with hospital consultants:

> Well, the consultants are all men. They are the most peculiar men too. When they don't get their own way they jump up and down and stamp their feet. I mean, they're like babies.
>
> [Q: How do you respond?]
>
> Well, there are some occasions you might deal with it and some occasions where you just say, 'oh well, that's that'. If I can possibly avoid consultants, I tend to do that. I'm not interested in that sort of reaction, but if I come face to face with them, and they say, 'look, this simply isn't good enough, you know, blah, blah, blah', I just say, 'well, this is what we do, this is what we've done, this is what we can do, and that's what I can offer, that's what social services can do'. Or I say, 'well, actually it's up to my managers not to me, go and see them if you want to', so I just say what my position is.
>
> (Gita)

> Well, I mean, of course the hospital hierarchy is, I mean, it is just so male dominated. It's very very white of course, it's very straight, it's very conservative, you know with a big 'C' and a little 'c' and I sometimes feel like a fish out of water.
>
> (Angela)

Links with voluntary organisations

The women social workers were more positive about links with voluntary sector organisations. They regarded the increased use of the voluntary sector as a significant development. They suggested three functions performed by the voluntary sector.

First, voluntary organisations were able to be more 'radical' than social workers in Social Services Departments, in terms of campaigning on behalf of service users:

> In a local authority, it is very difficult to be radical or pro-active. You have to work within, you don't move very far in the boundaries that have been set. The actual set-up doesn't allow you really to go for some big campaign of change. I think there may be some areas in children's services, like this family centre, that people can actually do something a little bit along those lines, but it's not going round with a banner. You need to go into the voluntary sector if you really want to campaign.
>
> (Amy)

> I mean it could better be done sometimes by an organisation not working within the constraints of local authority, local government.
>
> (Liza)

> Let's look maybe at taking it out of this arena, outside to the voluntary agency where, where you might be able to campaign or do something that's a bit more radical than what you can achieve within your agency.
>
> (Theresa)

Second, voluntary organisations were used to refer on work which fell outside definitions of 'core business', for example counselling, benefits advice, housing problems:

> You can refer on to the voluntary sector. You probably wouldn't be able to have the involvement yourself, but at least you'd have the satisfaction that you'd pointed people in the right direction to get some change.
>
> (Denise)

Finally, voluntary organisations were seen as more flexible and women-friendly:

> Often, agencies outside the SSD can be perceived as more women-friendly and have less of a power structure.
>
> (Ruth)

Feminist organisations and campaigns

The feminist social work literature has encouraged women social workers to involve themselves in feminist organisations and campaigns as an aspect of their practice (see Chapter 2): 'Women-only spaces and facilities have formed a radical feminist legacy that social workers have utilised in both practice and management. These are secure autonomous bases from which women can strategise and support one another, e.g., women in management groups, women in social work groups' (Dominelli 2002b: 27). Dominelli has suggested that such involvement enables women to 'play the insider–outsider role that provides a springboard for resistance to gender oppression' (ibid. 164). Barnes and Maple have emphasised that forms of radical practice cannot be developed in isolation from activity on a wider front (Barnes and Maple 1992: 143).

The women social workers were asked if they were involved in this type of wider front activity. Only two of them had such links. Both of these women were members of a local rape crisis centre. One of them was also engaged in a number of activities inside and outside her organisation that involved working with and representing women:

> I don't see it as political. It's a personal thing because, you know, the fact that somebody has been downtrodden in some way really sort of fires me. It's almost like if the department's saying, they've got an equal opps policy, let them put their money where their mouth is then, and if they're oppressing this particular person, then it could happen to any one of us, myself included.
>
> (Olive)

The remaining women social workers stated that they had no time or energy left over for wider front activities.

Women social workers and management

The examination of women social workers' experiences of managerialism now continues with a brief outline of issues pertaining to women and management and an exploration of the women social workers' stances on management. As we saw in Chapter 2, some feminist social work writers have argued that women social workers should seek promotion and engage with management agendas in order to advance women's interests:

> Management cannot be ignored by feminists. It is an important and strategic role and the site of power in every organisational setting. We must participate in it if women's priorities are ever to be equally represented and reflected in the structure of work.
>
> (Coyle, quoted in Everitt 1991: 135)

However, there have been considerable and longstanding barriers to women's participation in management: 'Social work should be the cause célèbre for women – a profession created by women for women. Yet in reality, women workers operate as the foot soldiers in an army governed by male generals' (Rojek *et al.* 1988: 7). This general pattern is well known and has been the subject of much attention in the feminist social work literature (see Chapter 2). At the time of the implementation of the Children Act 1989 and the NHS and Community Care Act 1990, the Social Services Inspectorate produced figures which showed that whilst 86 per cent of the workforce were women, they occupied only 18 per cent of senior positions and only 12 per cent of the directors of social services were women (Department of Health/Social Services Inspectorate 1991).

Ginn and Fisher's later findings continued to show that 'the more senior the management position, the less frequently it was occupied by women' and that 'despite the creation of many more English authorities by 1997, the proportion of women Directors remained the same' (Ginn and Fisher 1999: 130). Thus it has been argued that in spite of the widespread adoption of equal opportunities policies, Social Services Departments did not make significant inroads into the promotion of women in management (Newman 1995: 16). Whereas Harlow has argued that increasing managerialism has exacerbated women's under-representation in the senior management of Social Services Departments (Harlow 2004: 172), Dominelli has envisaged more women becoming managers in the future because the declining status of social work will result in fewer men entering the profession and competing for management posts (cited in Harlow 2004: 174).

In any case, given 'persistent and unending' gender inequality (Hughes 2002: 32), it is unlikely that a focus on numbers alone will be enough to bring about organisational change (Newman 1995: 11) in the direction of a feminisation of organisational culture. There seems little evidence in the women social workers' accounts of the 'feminisation of management' and the development of 'alternative ways of working with, and opening up the possibilities of change for, other women' (Newman 1995: 12). Wise's comment that everything would not change 'if all men left social work tomorrow' (Wise 1995: 116) seems particularly apposite with regard to management because

> organization and management . . . are inherently masculinist. That is, the preoccupation with order, control, instrumental rationality, hierarchy and domination are attributes of . . . masculinist apprehensions of how to be in the world . . . gender issues cannot be treated as secondary or additional but are absolutely centrally implicated.
>
> (Grey 2005: 127–8)

Being a manager

Those women social workers who were managers reflected on their experiences:

> I have to think about my own self-preservation and my own aspirations within this department and I know, regardless of what the equal opportunities policies say, that it's not good if your name gets known as a troublemaker.
>
> (Olive)

> I've got the challenge of being a woman manager with all male staff at the moment, apart from the clerk. Luckily, I had supervised male social workers already. It would have been very difficult, I think, coming here not having supervised any males. I mean, I did feel quite nervous coming in on the first day.
>
> (Amy)

> I worked in a totally female team in [X], and on the one hand, I mean, I was fresh out of college and I thought that was pretty good, you know, women together, we can change the world kind of thing, but when I came into youth justice I had to stand up for myself a lot more. The men took the view that, well, they appeared to take the view that they were more professional, that they could get on better with the police, you know. It was more buddy-buddy and they could deal with it and so to survive in the team I suppose I had to become more assertive, more self-confident, prove myself as a manager.*
> I think I had to work harder, to achieve the same level as they did.
>
> (Helen, *acting up as a manager)

The managers talked about hiding their emotions for fear of not being taken seriously in their organisations:

> There are times when being a women gets in the way of me challenging, I have to say that, and I mean that sounds like an odd thing to do from some-one who hardly finds it difficult to challenge at all, but there are times when I feel so strongly about something that I know that the way that I'm going to express it is going to be a very emotional way of expressing it and I choose not to express it because I don't want it to be dismissed as being an emotional response from a woman, so there are times, yes, when I won't challenge because I don't want the challenge to be dismissed I will have to think about it and find other ways of going back to that. I mean, I don't want people to see the tears in my eyes and not listen to the words, you know, and I'm sure that exists for some men as well, but it does prevent me from challenging.
>
> (Linda)

> I mean, I do get angry, mostly I get upset, and sometimes I have to come back to the office and I go into the toilet and have a bit of a cry. I'm not very good

at letting people see me getting upset, because you know there's this thing, over-involved, can't keep a good professional distance, so I'm a bit wary about that. So I have a bit of a cry and I come out and I think, right mate, I'll do something about this, and I might not be able to change the system, but I do believe in the dripping tap effect, and I think we can, we can have a positive input into individual people and to their families.

(Liza)

The experiences of these women square with Foster's comment that

Certain aspects of the corporate management culture are unattractive to many women who are critical of a culture of presenteeism rather than efficiency, of macho management styles, which emphasise competition as opposed to co-operation, and behaviour which focuses on self advancement rather than service enhancement.

(Quoted in Harlow 2004: 175)

Moving on to management

Four of the women social workers were already in management posts; two of them in child care and two in community care settings. Seven of the women were senior social workers in child care and one was a senior in community care. The remainder were social workers. The senior social workers and social workers were asked about whether they envisaged applying for managerial posts. Their responses fell into two categories. Three of them thought women were disadvantaged:

Lip service is given to equal opportunities, but accepted practice is, that women don't get managerial posts.

(Janis)

People I did my course with are all managers now. Women only apply for jobs if they think they can do them. Men apply for things that challenge them. Men just apply.

(Donna)

I was waiting, I suppose, for somebody to say, why don't you do this, and of course, that will never happen. But since branching out a bit myself, I've realised that I've got to take these opportunities myself. Nobody is going to come and say, 'Why don't you do the management training this year? It'll be just right for you'. Nobody has ever said that to me.

(Gaye)

The other type of response was a stress on a preference for and the importance of retaining contact with practice:

I wouldn't want to be a manager. I'm hooked on practice and the thing that keeps me going at the hospital are the patients because some of them are absolutely beautiful, and some of them I've absolutely adored and have seen that I've made a difference to them. I just really like working with clients.

(Angela)

I'm drawn more to therapeutic work than to management. If you look at the way things are going you just get de-skilled.

(Donna)

I don't think management is for me. I've recently had a crack at it. Our team manager went, moved up one, and I moved into his shoes, and I suppose I've always felt a sense, I've assumed that being in a managerial position that you lose contact with practice completely, that the function that you undertake bears no reality at all to any evidence from practice and I was able to test that out. It's absolutely true.

(Theresa)

For Theresa and Angela their concerns about being removed from practice were combined with anxiety about having to make personal compromises in order to accommodate to the management culture:

We're split on two floors. The manager never came to see upstairs people and I often said to him, 'you ought to come upstairs and have a cup of coffee with us, we want to see you', but he never did. Then, when I was in that position myself,* in what had been his room, I got a sense of, gosh, I must get upstairs today because I haven't seen anybody and I've got to do it, and it was a conscious thought that I had to keep with me otherwise I would not have done it. You could be behind that door and nobody would ever know you're there. I hated that. It's just something about the role that cuts you off. And so I'm glad really that I didn't take that on permanently. It still wouldn't interest me. You know, I'd be stuck behind that thing all day [points to computer] and in meetings. But the meetings, again, are so far from the reality of everyday work.

(Theresa, * acting up as a manager)

If I'm being very honest, I'm far too controlling to be a manager. I'd want people to come in on time, and I'd want people to be accountable, and I'd want to know that they've done a good job, so I'd make their lives miserable and I'd make my own life miserable.

(Angela)

Three of the women thought that career advancement depended on the possession of 'managerial assets' (Causer and Exworthy 1999: 99) and had enrolled on external management courses in the hope that being associated with what was seen as the discrete and privileged body of managerialist knowledge would lead to their promotion:

> I hope to apply for a senior's job in this team. I hope to get a serious academic qualification now I've started on this route, so I'd like to. I don't like to say anything in words in case I never achieve it really, but I'd quite like to do the MBA eventually. So yes, if our senior moves on, then I might apply, or even might apply for the team manager's job. I wish I had done this training ten years ago.
>
> (Gaye)

> At the moment I'm doing management, postgraduate management at [X] University, so I'm keeping abreast of all the changes. I would like to go into management at some stage.
>
> (Zina)

> I'm doing a course in my own time, a course on management, to help with doing this job and for my own personal development really. I asked [X] if the course was available through our staff development section. They have got access to a Diploma in Management Studies course run through the central personnel department. I didn't realise that it was still available but, I mean, I couldn't have the time out to do it, so there was no point in asking really.
>
> (Amy)

These women's experiences accorded with a general trend that has been identified by a number of writers who have argued that increased managerialism has resulted in experience of social work practice no longer being sufficient to become a manager. This has resulted in the certification of management in its own right through accredited management training courses (Harlow 1998; Dominelli and Hoogvelt 1996; Healy 2002). However, as Harlow has pointed out

> Many women, particularly older women, still say caring responsibilities inhibit investment in their career. As a consequence, participation in such courses will be difficult unless employers allocate adequate study leave. Financial constraints within SSDs, as well as staff shortages, hinder the possibility of this occurring.
>
> (Harlow 2004: 174)

Even if women are successful in securing support to attend management courses, the masculinist values that they experience as pervading the organisational cultures in which they work are replicated in management training provision: 'not only does management education validate values of control and domination but it also uses case studies of predominantly male leaders and, in the classroom, routinely silences or discounts the contributions of female students' (Grey 2005: 114).

Conclusion

We have seen that the women social workers found ways of accommodating to the negative features of managerialism and to a limited extent were able to challenge them. However, there was a strong sense of managerialism's reinforcement of men's power over resources and decision-making and the disempowering of social workers in the context of a 'woman's profession' that is largely controlled by men (Dominelli 2002b: 42). The women social workers suggested that simply having women in management does not necessarily change the masculinist organisational culture. The existing women managers expressed their sense of estrangement from this culture. Some of the women social workers saw themselves as potential managers and had pursued courses that would lead in that direction. The majority of these women saw practice as the focal point for any work that was considered to be worthwhile and, in that respect, echoed the heavy emphasis on face-to-face practice in the feminist social work literature (see Chapter 1).

Chapter 10

The state of feminist social work

The book has provided an account of the feminist social work academic literature and has followed up points of tension between that literature's proposals for feminist practice and women social workers' descriptions of their experiences. In exploring the tensions between the literature and women social workers' experiences, the dominant perspective in the literature has been questioned, namely that women social workers in state social work can align themselves with a feminist identity and engage in egalitarian relationships with women service users, with the goal of empowerment. In contrast to the dominant perspective, the book has demonstrated the existence of diverse identities, identifications and stances amongst women social workers. The only consistent aspect was that none of the participants primarily aligned themselves with a feminist identity as a stance from which to approach their work. The majority of the participants were, in their own terms, seeking to use principles they perceived as being derived from feminism, with varying degrees of attachment to the term 'feminist' itself. 'Feminist' had stronger support as a term that indicated their commitment to women's interests within an overarching notion of anti-discriminatory and/or anti-oppressive practice, than it did as a term of self-identity and self-identification. Langan's (1992a) and Wise's (1995) formulations of anti-discriminatory practice capture the stances of the majority of the participants more effectively than the proposals of the dominant perspective in the feminist social work literature.

With regard to the literature's proposal concerning the creation of egalitarian relationships with women service users, the women social workers saw this as not being feasible (see Chapter 8). It was possible to infer a level of unacknowledged shared experience with women service users on the part of the women social workers but this fell well short of the possibility of egalitarian relationships and might be more appropriately referred to as latent empathy. There was a similar lack of evidence for the existence of empowerment. Instead, participants endorsed the employment of a more modest concept of empowerment in terms of service user participation. Partnership with service users was identified as a concrete expression of empowerment but this was seen as problematic, indicating some of the difficulties that were experienced in realising even the more modest mandate of participation, within the constraints of state social work practice. The explicit expectations and anticipated outcomes of partnership appeared to lead social workers away from the abstract principles and rhetorical flourishes of empowerment found in the literature and back into the dilemmas and constraints of state social work.

State social work

The book has brought state social work into the foreground and provided a more detailed elaboration of it than that found in the feminist social work literature. Within the literature's dominant perspective, the proposals for feminist social work are concerned with what women social workers' practice *ought to be like*, but the women social workers' experiences have shown that this formulation of feminist social work is detached from an understanding of the nature of state social work *as it is*. The elaboration of state social work as a state-mediated profession, operating in and through a bureau-professional regime, was thus an essential corrective to the lacuna in the dominant perspective. Providing an analytical framework for state social work not only contextualised the experiences of women social workers but also revealed that their room for manoeuvre in influencing the nature of their practice with women service users lay in the means by which they undertook the state's legislatively defined ends of their work. In contrast, we saw that, in much of the feminist social work literature, women social workers have been presented as making choices about the ends, as well as the means, of their work with women service users and are thus seen as possessing the autonomy to transcend the implementation of statutory duties on the state's behalf. In retrospect, it can be seen that the major contributions to the feminist social work literature (see Chapters 1 and 2) were formulated at a time when there was more professional 'space' within the social democratic welfare state (see Chapters 3 and 4). This allowed women social workers to have a substantial degree of control over their day-to-day work (and see Harris 2003: 14–24). The discretion they enjoyed allowed the possibility of experimenting with feminist approaches to practice. Similarly, there was academic 'space' in that the major contributions to the feminist social work literature emerged at a time when there were no stipulations concerning the content of the social work curriculum (see Chapter 5). Both of these spaces have been pressurised by the incursion of managerialism into organisation, practice and education (see Chapters 4, 5 and 9). The women social workers' accounts indicated the extent to which they perceived their discretion over the means of undertaking their work had been eroded.

The process of constraining discretion began under the Conservative governments but, from the outset, New Labour's agenda continued to close down openings for feminist social work of the kind envisaged in the dominant perspective in the feminist social work literature. *Modernising Social Services* (Department of Health 1998), *Modern Local Government* (Department of the Environment, Transport and the Regions 1998) and the *Performance Assessment Framework* (Department of Health 1999) established systems of closer scrutiny and more interventionist management of performance by central government that sharpened the focus on the consistency of processes and outcomes and levels of achievement against specific criteria. For example, the Commission for Social Care Inspection has been using such approaches to judge local authorities on how well they are currently providing social services, rating them from nought to three stars, and on how likely the services are to improve. The reports on local authorities show how services inspected compare with those of other authorities. This instrumental approach does not seem conducive to the development of feminist social work, as presented in the dominant perspective in the feminist social work literature. Given the developments that have restricted the room for manoeuvre within state social work, the realisation of the dominant perspective's model of feminist social work appears to face insurmountable difficulties. If this were the case, there seem to be three options: opting out, co-option and being in and against managerialism.

Opting out

Women social workers could opt out of state social work in one of three ways: by continuing to promote an unrealisable version of feminist social work in state social work; by simply giving up on seeking to advance women's interests; by focusing on feminist initiatives outside state social work, given the argument that the statutory context closes off specifically feminist ends for social work (Wise 1995).

Co-option

Co-option can occur either because women social workers internalise managerialism unwittingly or as they align themselves with it instrumentally. In both cases, they can become its uncritical agents. Postle (2001) has suggested that one of the strategies practitioners have employed to cope with the changing nature of their work has been no longer to challenge or question 'inherent dissonances'. Drawing on the work of Lipsky (1980), Postle maintains that this approach involves practitioners adopting a 'client-processing mentality' through which they 'psychologically adapt themselves to their jobs in order to cope with dissonances . . . This approach lends itself to an apparent willingness to follow procedural models of working' (Postle 2001: 20).

In and against managerialism

Social work is in a relatively and increasingly subordinate position within the state (Webb 1996: 163; Jones 2001; Harris 2003) that would appear to render increasingly redundant the dominant perspective's proposals for an alternative, self-generated, feminist approach to practice. A way forward, proposed by Langan (1992a) and Wise (1995), would be attempting to further women's interests, when and where possible, under the guise of anti-discriminatory or anti-oppressive practice. Feminist social work seems to have been increasingly incorporated within this framework. Practice principles for anti-oppressive social work are remarkably similar to those found in the feminist social work literature. For example, Dominelli states that anti-oppressive practice is

> A form of social work practice which addresses social divisions and structural inequalities in the work that is done with clients (users) or workers. AOP aims to provide more appropriate and sensitive services by responding to people's needs regardless of their social status. AOP embodies a person-centred philosophy, an egalitarian value system concerned with reducing the deleterious effects of structural inequalities upon people's lives; a methodology focusing on process and outcome; and a way of structuring social relationships between individuals that aims to empower service users by reducing the negative effects of hierarchy in their immediate interaction and the work they do.
>
> (Dominelli quoted in Healy 2005: 179)

However, it has been argued that anti-oppressive/anti-discriminatory practice has been incorporated by the state and has

> allowed the state to reposition itself as a benign arbiter between competing identity claims. Perversely, given its aim to make the personal political, it has allowed the problems of society to be recast as due to moral failings of individuals who need censure and correction from the anti-oppressive social worker . . . the anti-oppressive social worker is well placed for personally policing, not politically empowering, the disadvantaged.
>
> (McLaughlin 2005: 300)

In this context, Sakamato and Pitner have argued for greater clarity about what anti-oppressive practice entails:

> Does it refer to a social worker's attempt to eliminate racism, sexism, classism on behalf of service users? Does it refer to a social worker's attempt to eliminate any isms in working collaboratively with service users? Does it refer to an attempt to eliminate power differentials across the board? . . . For some social workers, radical social work and anti-oppressive practice may mean the same thing, whereas for others, empowerment approaches may be regarded as part of anti-oppressive practice.
>
> (Sakamato and Pitner 2005: 437)

This debate about the dual potential (progressive and incorporative) of anti-oppressive practice illustrates some of the difficulties of occupying a position of being in and against managerialism. However, such an approach recognises the defining characteristics of state social work and offers women social workers a means of seeing through their jobs in ways that acknowledge the circumstances in which they find themselves. Whilst the continuing influence of managerialism is undeniable it may be possible to interrupt and disturb it at some points. This would seem to accord with the women social workers' presentation of their identities as more ambivalent and ambiguous than those presented in the feminist social work literature but as still reflecting agendas that went beyond succumbing completely, and unthinkingly, to managerialism. For example, we saw evidence that despite the codification and computerisation of social work, the responses of women social workers were not completely programmed; managerialism requires responses to service users that draw to some extent upon women social workers' interpretations and the use of their judgement. The managerial objectives of social work cannot be achieved by the simple imposition of bureaucratic regulations. Categorising need and meeting it with a standardised response is rarely sufficient for the completion of social work tasks (Lymbery 1998: 876) and an element of continued discretion is still required, even in managerialised bureau-professional regimes (Evans and Harris 2004). Reliance on the informal negotiation of solutions to problems, with imposed formal solutions only as the last resort (Jordan 1987, 1990), can still be defended as a key aspect of social work.

Conclusion

Opening up these sorts of considerations begins to question a view of managerialism that assumes it has been smoothly and effectively implemented, that social workers have met its requirements completely and that they have no influence over its effects. It also begins to suggest that there may be areas in which women social workers can exercise some influence on developments. Three such examples can be provided.

First, considerable numbers of women have moved into middle and front-line management positions. This makes it difficult to continue to refer to managerialism as something that is being imposed upon women by men. This is not to suggest that a straightforward take-over by women is in progress. As we saw in Chapter 9, the masculinist managerial frames of reference are still experienced as being largely intact and the commanding heights of managerial hierarchies are still dominated by men. However, the increased involvement of women in management does hold out the possibility of the development of organisational regimes in which the debates about whether and how social work can address women's interests will be between women at the same and different levels in those regimes, rather than being articulated in circumstances involving the male managerial subordination of women in vertically gender-segregated organisations.

Second, strategies at the team level were the subject of considerable discussion in the radical social work era (see, for example, Bailey and Brake 1975; Corrigan and Leonard 1978), but such debates have now disappeared from view. Yet, as we saw in the last chapter, to an even greater extent than is the case more generally in state social work's organisational regimes, social work teams are becoming women's zones. The devolution of managerial responsibilities to these zones has been accompanied by remote, computerised surveillance of their work (Harris 2003: 64–75). However, they are, in day-to-day terms, increasingly isolated islands of service delivery, with a measure of detachment from senior managers and managerial surveillance systems.

Third, managerialism exerts increasing pressure to 'deliver' on services, for example under the guise of quality assurance or risk management. There may be opportunities for women to re-cast their goals in terms such as these, which managerialism recognises and which fall under its agendas. There are glimpses of such possibilities, with women social workers identifying a more equitable approach to practice, the encouragement of service users' participation and the development of 'good practice' within managerialism's agenda (White and Harris 2001, 2004). Postle has referred to the exploitation of opportunities for working against the constraints of managerialism as 'undercover work' (Postle 2001: 21). Lymbery has suggested an approach through which such undercover work might be surfaced and result in changes to practice:

> Practitioners must develop ways of articulating the importance of their work – and of justifying their actions – within a managerialist frame of reference. They must also become actively involved in more proactive, preventive work, as a means of counterbalancing the crisis-led approach characterising much statutory work. The key to this is to work simultaneously at two separate levels. On the one hand, social workers need to perform the tasks that are required of them to establish their credibility as skilled practitioners. On the other, they should identify the limitations of these approaches and press for alternative ways of conceptualising how services should be organised.
>
> (Lymbery 2001: 380)

Only on the basis of thorough analysis will we know whether alternative ways of conceptualising and organising services in the interests of women are possible. Such an analysis of the potential for change would contain tensions between pragmatism and principle and would need to focus on political, policy and practice contingencies. In other words, it would be an analysis of contextualised power relations (Wise 1995: 104, 116) that would need to be realistic and specific (Langan and Lee 1989: 8–9, 14) about what is possible in connecting state social work with women's interests.

Identifying the possibilities for resistance to the dominant discourse of managerialism is consistent with the core place that has been accorded to resistance in documenting, theorising and researching workplace cultures and behaviour (Thomas and Davies 2005). Thomas and Davies suggest that ideas about resistance have been extended beyond a narrow focus on the collective activities of oppressed women towards a wider appreciation of resistance as multifaceted. This opens up a view of resistance that does not have to be synonymous with large-scale transformation, as depicted in the dominant perspective in the feminist social work literature, but can encompass a range of challenges by women social workers, working in and against managerialism for more critical forms of practice that seek to engage with furthering women's interests.

Sampling, interviewing and data analysis

Sampling

With the agreement of the director of a practice teaching programme and a senior manager, who had line management responsibility on behalf of the consortium of Social Services Departments involved in the programme, I wrote to the 42 women who had completed the programme and were still employed in their sponsoring departments. I asked if they had an interest in women's perspectives on social work and whether they would be interested in being interviewed. Twenty identified themselves as having an interest in participating in the interviews. Thus, the sample was purposive and self-selecting.

The participants in the interviews were asked for biographical details about themselves: their age, ethnic origin, sexual orientation, whether or not they had a physical impairment, length of time in social work, current job and area of practice in social work. This information is provided in Appendix II.

Interviews

Semi-structured interviews were used in which the topics to be covered were predetermined. A flexible approach was adopted in order to allow modifications to be made to the interviews as they progressed, following the flow of the discussion. This style of interviewing was adopted in order to engage the participants in the construction of the data – 'telling it like it is' (Graham 1984: 105) – rather than operating on the assumption that themes from the literature should determine the course of the interview (Finch 1984; Graham 1983; Oakley 1981). It seemed reasonable to anticipate that using such an approach in interviews with women social workers would allow access to their accounts of their experiences in state social work.

Interviewing arrangements

All of the interviews lasted for at least one hour. The majority took place in the participants' workplaces. Only one of the participants asked to meet outside of the work setting and this was for her convenience. In advance of the interview the participants were sent a letter outlining the nature of my interests. I summarised the areas to be covered at the beginning of each interview to try and ensure that each participant was confident that there were no hidden agendas. I also used this as an opportunity to stress that I was interested in the interview being used as a vehicle for their accounts of their experiences. I assured them that their anonymity would be preserved when the data were written up. All of the participants agreed to the tape recording of their interviews. Following the interviews, typed copies of transcripts were sent to participants for checking and additional comments were invited. Five participants responded by correcting minor transcription errors. No-one added any additional information.

Data analysis

After transcribing the tapes, the initial ordering of the data was accomplished by listening to the tape of each interview until a sense of the whole interview was attained and then its structure and its themes were mapped out. After this mapping on an interview by interview basis, I listened to the tapes again. This time I focused on the detail within the themes and divided the transcripts into sections which were collated across the interviews. I had some preconceptions about the categories for analysing the data, generated from the themes in the literature. However, I was also aware of these categories being amended by other themes emerging from the participants. For example, the language they used to describe the type of social work in which they were engaged and its relationship to new managerialism.

Appendix II

Profile of the women social workers

Name	Age	Ethnicity	Physical impairment	Sexuality	Years of social work experience	Current post	Area of work
Linda	46	UK European	No	Heterosexual	26	Manager	Community care
Candy	34	UK European	No	Heterosexual	12	Social worker	Community care
Cindy	33	UK European	No	Heterosexual	11	Senior social worker	Children's services
Hilary	37	Asian	No	Heterosexual	14	Senior social worker	Children's services
Olive	42	African-Caribbean	No	Heterosexual	20	Manager	Children's services
Theresa	56	UK European	No	Heterosexual	26	Senior social worker	Community care
Zina	45	East African Asian	No	Heterosexual	7	Social worker	Children's services
Liza	43	UK European	No	Heterosexual	17	Manager	Children's services
Ruth	47	UK European	No	Heterosexual	5	Social worker	Children's services
Donna	34	Ugandan African	No	Heterosexual	14	Senior social worker	Children's services
Janis	42	UK European	No	Heterosexual	20	Senior social worker	Children's services
Gaye	41	UK European	No	Heterosexual	17	Social worker	Both
Anita	51	UK European	No	Heterosexual	28	Senior social worker	Children's services
Elsie	50	UK European	No	Heterosexual	7	Social worker	Community care
Iris	32	UK European	No	Heterosexual	9	Senior social worker	Children's services
Gita	50	UK European	No	Heterosexual	15	Social worker	Community care
Helen	45	UK European	No	Heterosexual	15	Senior social worker	Children's services
Angela	43	UK European	Yes	Lesbian	25	Social worker	Community care
Amy	42	UK European	No	Heterosexual	18	Manager	Community care
Denise	30	UK European	No	Lesbian	4	Social worker	Child care

Notes

1 Feminist social work identity

1 An exception to the eclectic approach is Comley's socialist-feminist contribution, which sees feminist social work in statutory settings as combining class antagonism and gender conflict: 'State services cannot be comprehended as unambiguously benign, nor as unequivocally oppressive. Rather, they constitute a contradictory unity which lends itself to analysis through reference to socialist and feminist theory. These theoretical frameworks reveal the state as a site of struggle and can be used to elucidate the structural location of state employees in this dynamic, as well as identifying the extent to which it is possible to implement practices which will challenge the state's oppressive tendencies' (Comley 1989: 58).

2 Egalitarian relationships, empowerment and statutory social work

1 In this example, not only are the power relationships within which social workers operate rendered invisible, but also women social workers are presented as autonomous decision-makers, choosing how they want to work with women service users. (The shortcomings in this representation of statutory social work will be considered on page 25 and in chapter 3.)

2 The exceptions are Hale (1984) and Wise (1985, 1995).

3 They also refer to Hale's (1984) work.

3 State social work

1 This bleak depiction of the functioning of social work cautions against glib use of the term 'empowerment': 'Subjects are constructed . . . in discourses, including discourses of organisation, in a way that enables a subject's actions to become meaningful, a mode of objectification that provides the ground where power/resistance takes a beneficial turn and can lead to empowerment of the subject. Empowerment is not easily gained, of course, because resistance to the power of dominant discourse is everywhere opposed, and we can assume that organisation will attempt to suppress and eliminate resistance through the various techniques of subjectification (diagnosis, classification, exclusive professional language, surveillance, medication, therapy) which organisation has available' (Leonard 1997a: 92). An example of such processes in relation to community care settings is provided by Means and Smith, who refer to 'assessment, diagnosis, screening, codification and categorisation, all of which serve to help define the client, and the nature of his or her problems, in technical, legislative and bureaucratic terms' (Means and Smith 1998: 74).

4 Social work regimes

1   The position of Social Services Departments as the main sites of state social work is changing with the merging of social services for children with education provision in Children's Trusts (Children Act 2004).

5 Social work education

1   Later in the chapter, the significance of this intervention by directors of Social Services Departments in shaping partnership as one of the key dimensions of change in the 1990s will become clear.
2   The revised *Paper 30* (CCETSW 1991a) added language, sign language and nationality.
3   Competence is discussed further on pages 68–69.
4   Partnership is discussed further on pages 69–71.
5   The NCVQ terms are given first, followed by the Diploma in Social Work terms in brackets.
6   Again, this perhaps illustrates the influence of the NCVQ framework that treated anti-discriminatory practice in an individualised and personalised way.
7   'Gender and sexuality are presumably included in 'other difference'.
8   Given the influence of the National Council for Vocational Qualifications (NCVQ) framework on CCETSW's proposals perhaps a definition from the NCVQ could be substituted as a working definition: 'The ability to perform work activities to the standards required in employment' (NCVQ 1988: 2).
9   The GSCC is the body for England. The other bodies are the Scottish Social Services Council, the Care Council for Wales and the Northern Ireland Social Care Council.

7 Egalitarian relationships and empowerment in practice

1   The use of the word 'female' here and elsewhere in the chapter may indicate a sense of distance, at this point from students and later in the chapter from women service users, with the latter sometimes referred to as simply 'females' (see the discussion in the Conclusion to the chapter, page 109).
2   This provides empirical support for the position mentioned in Chapter 1, namely that 'the assumption is that gender issues are addressed by virtue of the presence of a predominantly female workforce and clientele' (Dominelli 1991: 183).

8 Managerialism and practice

1   Of course, a key aspect of the difference in the process is social workers' more direct involvement in rationing resources than was the case previously (see Chapter 4).
2   This comment is consistent with the finding in another study of the varying extent to which managerial agendas had been incorporated into different teams (Ellis *et al*. 1999).
3   'Pick-lists' are pre-formatted categories from which social workers have to choose designations for service users' problems and their responses to them.

Bibliography

Adams, R. (1998) 'Social work processes', in R. Adams, L. Dominelli and M. Payne (eds) *Social Work: Themes, Issues and Critical Debates*, Basingstoke: Macmillan.

Aldridge, M. (1996) 'Dragged to market: being a profession in the postmodern world', *British Journal of Social Work*, 26: 177–194.

Ang, I. (1995) 'I'm a feminist but . . .: "other" women and post-national feminism', in B. Caine and R. Pringle (eds) *Transitions: New Australian Feminisms*, Sydney: Allen and Unwin.

Anleu, S. L. (1992) 'The professionalisation of social work? A case study of three organisational settings', *Sociology*, 26, 1: 23–43.

Appleyard, B. (1993) 'Why paint so black a picture?' *Independent*, 4 August.

Asfar, H. and Maynard, M. (1994) *The Dynamics of 'Race' and Gender: Some Feminist Interventions*, London: Taylor and Francis.

Audit Commission (1988) *The Competitive Council*, London: HMSO.

Aymer, C. (1992) 'Women in residential work: dilemmas and ambiguities', in M. Langan and L. Day (eds) *Women, Oppression and Social Work: Issues in Anti-discriminatory Practice*, London: Routledge.

Bailey, R. and Brake, M. (eds) (1975) *Radical Social Work*, London: Edward Arnold.

Balen, R., Brown, K. and Taylor, C. (1993) 'It seems so much is expected of us: practice teachers, the DipSW and anti-discriminatory practice', *Issues in Social Work Education*, 12, 3: 17–40.

Banks, S. (1998) 'Professional ethics in social work – what future ?' *British Journal of Social Work*, 28: 213–231.

Barnes, M. and Maple, N. (1992) *Women and Mental Health: Challenging the Stereotypes*, Birmingham: Venture Press.

Begum, N. (1994) *Reflections: The Views of Black Disabled People on their Lives and Community Care (Paper 32.3)*, London: Central Council for Education and Training in Social Work.

Begum, N. (1995) *Beyond Samosas and Reggae: A Guide to Developing Services for Black Disabled People*, London: Kings Fund.

Birmingham Women and Social Work Group (1985) 'Women and social work in Birmingham', in E. Brook and A. Davis (eds) *Women, the Family and Social Work*, London: Tavistock.

Blair, T. (1998) *The Third Way: New Politics for the New Century*, London: The Fabian Society.

Braye, S. and Preston-Shoot, M. (1995) *Empowering Practice in Social Care*, Buckingham: Open University Press.

Braye, S. and Preston-Shoot, M. (1998) 'Social work and the law', in R. Adams, L. Dominelli and M. Payne (eds) *Social Work: Themes, Issues and Critical Debates*, Basingstoke: Macmillan.

Brewster, R. (1992) 'The new class? Managerialism and social work education and training', *Issues in Social Work Education*, 2, 2: 81–93.

Brook, E. and Davis, A. (1985a) 'Afterword', in E. Brook and A. Davis (eds) *Women, the Family and Social Work*, London: Tavistock.

Brook, E. and Davis, A. (1985b) 'Introduction', in E. Brook and A. Davis (eds) *Women, the Family and Social Work*, London: Tavistock.

Bryan, A. (1992) 'Working with black single mothers: myths and reality', in M. Langan and L. Day (eds) *Women, Oppression and Social Work: Issues in Anti-discriminatory Practice*, London: Routledge.

Bryan, B., Dadzie, S. and Scafe, S. (1985) *The Heart of the Race: Black Women's Lives in Britain*, London: Virago.

Buckle, J. (1981) *Intake Teams*, London: Tavistock.

Burke, B. and Harrison, P. (1998) 'Anti-oppressive practice', in R. Adams, L. Dominelli and M. Payne (eds) *Social Work: Themes, Issues and Critical Debates*, Basingstoke, Macmillan.

Butler, I. and Drakeford, M. (2001a) 'Which Blair project? Communitarianism, social authoritarianism and social work', *Journal of Social Work*, 1, 1: 7–19.

Butler, I. and Drakeford, M. (2001b) 'Editorial', *British Journal of Social Work*, 30, 1: 1–2.

Butler, S. and Wintram, C. (1991) *Feminist Groupwork*, London: Sage.

Cannan, C. (1994/5) 'Enterprise culture, professional socialisation, and social work education in Britain', *Critical Social Policy*, 14, 3: 5–18.

Carby, H. (1982) 'White women listen! Black feminism and the boundaries of sisterhood', in Centre for Contemporary Cultural Studies, *The Empire Strikes Back*, London: Hutchinson.

Carter, P., Everrit, A. and Hughes, A. (1992) 'Malestream training? Women, feminism and social work education', in M. Langan and L. Day (eds) *Women, Oppression and Social Work*, London: Routledge.

Causer, G. and Exworthy, M. (1999) 'Professionals as managers across the public sector', in M. Exworthy and S. Halford (eds) *Professionals and the New Managerialism in the Public Sector*, Buckingham: Open University Press.

Cavanagh, K. and Cree, V. (1996) *Working with Men: Feminism and Social Work*, London: Routledge.

CCETSW (1977) *Consultative Document 3: Patterns of Education and Training Leading to the Certificate of Qualification in Social Work. Policy Issues Arising from Consultative Documents 1 and 2*, London: Central Council for Education and Training in Social Work.

CCETSW (1983) *Review of Qualifying Training Policies, Paper 20*, London: Central Council for Education and Training in Social Work.

CCETSW (1986) *Paper 20.6: Three Years and Different Routes. Council's Expectations and Intentions for Social Work Training*, London: Central Council for Education and Training in Social Work.

CCETSW (1987) *Care for Tomorrow*, London: Central Council for Education and Training in Social Work.

CCETSW (1989) *Paper 30: Rules and Requirements for the Diploma in Social Work*, London: Central Council for Education and Training in Social Work.

CCETSW (1990) *Partnerships and Collaboration in Programmes for the Diploma in Social Work. A Guidance Note on Paper 30*, London: Central Council for Education and Training in Social Work.

CCETSW (1991a) *Revised Paper 30: Rules and Requirements for the Diploma in Social Work*, London: Central Council for Education and Training in Social Work.

CCETSW (1991b) *Paper 26.3: Improving Standards in Practice Learning Requirements and Guidance for the Approval of Agencies and the Accreditation and Training of Practice Teachers*, London: Central Council for Education and Training in Social Work.

CCETSW (1994) *Diploma in Social Work: Update One*, London: Central Council for Education and Training in Social Work.

CCETSW (1995a) *Assuring Quality in the Diploma in Social Work 1: Rules and Requirements for the DipSW*, London: Central Council for Education and Training in Social Work.

CCETSW (1995b) *CCETSW News No. 2*, London: Central Council for Education and Training in Social Work.

Challis, L. (1990) *Organising Public Social Services*, London: Longman.

Charles, N. (2000) *Feminism, the State and Social Policy*, Basingstoke: Macmillan.

Christie, A. (2001) 'Gendered discourses of welfare, men and social work', in A. Christie (ed.) *Men and Social Work: Theories and Practice*, Basingstoke Palgrave.

Clarke, J. (1979) 'Critical sociology and radical social work: problems of theory and practice', in N. Parry, M. Rustin and C. Satyamurti (eds) *Social Work, Welfare and the State*, London: Edward Arnold.

Clarke, J. (2005) 'New Labour's citizens: activated, empowered, responsibilized, abandoned?' *Critical Social Policy*, 25, 4: 447–463.

Clarke, J., Cochrane, A. and McLaughlin, E. (eds) (1994) *Managing Social Policy*, London: Sage.

Clarke, J. and Langan, M. (1993) 'Restructuring welfare: the British welfare regime in the 1980s', in A. Cochrane and J. Clarke (eds) *Comparing Welfare States: Britain in International Context*, London: Sage.

Clarke, J. and Newman, J. (1993) 'Managing to survive: dilemmas of changing organisational forms in the public sector', in N. Deakin and R. Page (eds) *The Costs of Welfare*, Aldershot: Avebury.

Clarke, J. and Newman, J. (1997) *The Managerial State*, London: Sage.

Cohen, M. and Mullender, A. (2003) *Gender and Groupwork*, London: Routledge.

Comley, T. (1989) 'State social work: a socialist-feminist contribution', in C. Hallett (ed.) *Women and Social Services Departments*, Hemel Hempstead: Harvester Wheatsheaf.

Cooper, J. (1991) 'The future of social work: a pragmatic view', in M. Loney, R. Bocock, J. Clarke, A. Cochrane, P. Graham and M. Wilson (eds) *The State or the Market: Politics and Welfare in Contemporary Britain*, London: Sage.

Corby, B. (1993) *Child Abuse: Towards a Knowledge Base*, Buckingham: Open University Press.

Corrigan, P. and Leonard, P. (1978) *Social Work Practice under Capitalism: A Marxist Approach*, London: Macmillan.

Cosis-Brown, H. (1992) 'Lesbians, the state and social work practice', in M. Langan and L. Day (eds) *Women's Oppression and Social Work: Issues in Anti-discriminatory Practice*, London: Routledge.

Cosis-Brown, H. (1998) 'Counselling', in R. Adams, L. Dominelli and M. Payne (eds) *Social Work: Themes, Issues and Critical Debates*, Basingstoke: Macmillan.

Cousins, C. (1987) *Controlling Social Welfare*, Brighton: Wheatsheaf.

Cree, V. (2001) 'Men and masculinities in social work education', in A. Christie (ed.) *Men and Social Work: Theories and Practice*, Basingstoke: Palgrave.

CSCI (Commission for Social Care Inspection) (2005) Online. Available HTTP: <http://www.csci.org.uk/csci_or_chai.htm>. Accessed 18 October.

Dale, J. and Foster, P. (1986) *Feminists and State Welfare*, London: Routledge & Kegan Paul.

Dalrymple, J. and Burke, B. (1995) *Anti-oppressive Practice: Social Care and the Law*, Buckingham: Open University Press.

Davies, M. (1986) *The Essential Social Worker*, Aldershot: Gower.

Davis, A. (1996) 'Women and the personal social services', in C. Hallett (ed.) *Women and Social Policy: An Introduction*, Hemel Hempstead: Harvester Wheatsheaf.

Davis, A. and Brook, E. (1985) 'Women and social work', in E. Brook and A. Davis (eds) *Women, the Family and Social Work*, London: Tavistock.

Day, L. (1992) 'Women and oppression: race, class and gender', in M. Langan and L. Day (eds) *Women, Oppression and Social Work. Issues in Anti-discriminatory Practice*, London: Routledge.

Department of the Environment, Transport and the Regions (1998) *Modern Local Government: In Touch with the People*, London: Stationery Office.

Department of Health (1989) *Community Care in the Next Decade and Beyond*, London: HMSO.

Department of Health (1990) *Community Care in the Next Decade and Beyond: Policy Guidance*, London: HMSO.

Department of Health (1998) *Modernising Social Services*, London: HMSO.

Department of Health (1999) *A New Approach to Social Services Performance: Consultation Document*, London: Department of Health.

Department of Health (2000) *A Quality Strategy for Social Care*, London: HMSO.

Department of Health (2002) *Requirements for Social Work Training*, London: Department of Health.

Department of Health/Social Services Inspectorate (1991) *Women in Social Services: A Neglected Resource*, London: HMSO.

Derber, C. (1982) 'Managing professionals: ideological proletarianization and mental labor', in C. Derber (ed.) *Professionals as Workers: Mental Labor in Advanced Capitalism*, Boston: G.K. Hall.

Derber, C. (1983) 'Managing professionals: ideological proletarianization and post-industrial labor', *Theory and Society*, 12, 3: 309–341.

Dominelli, L (1991) '"Race", gender and social work', in M. Davies (ed.) *The Sociology of Social Work*, London: Routledge.

Dominelli, L. (1992) 'More than a method: feminist social work', in K. Campbell (ed.) *Critical Feminism: Argument in the Disciplines*, Buckingham: Open University Press.

Dominelli, L. (1996) 'Deprofessionalising social work: anti-oppressive practice, competencies and post-modernism', *British Journal of Social Work*, 26, 2: 153–175.

Dominelli, L. (1997) *Sociology for Social Work*, Basingstoke: Macmillan.

Dominelli, L. (1998a) 'Feminist social work: an expression of universal human rights', *Indian Journal of Social Work*, 59, 4: 917–929.

Dominelli, L. (1998b) 'Anti-oppressive practice in context', in R. Adams, L. Dominelli and M. Payne (eds) *Social Work: Themes, Issues and Critical Debates*, Basingstoke: Macmillan.

Dominelli, L. (2002a) 'Feminist theory', in M. Davies (ed.) *The Blackwell Companion to Social Work*, 2nd edn, Oxford: Blackwell.

Dominelli, L. (2002b) *Feminist Social Work Theory and Practice*, Basingstoke: Palgrave.

Dominelli, L. (2002c) *Anti-oppressive Social Work Theory and Practice*, London: Palgrave.

Dominelli, L. and Hoogvelt, A. (1996) 'Globalization and the technocratization of social work', *Critical Social Policy*, 16, 2: 45–62.

Dominelli, L. and McLeod, E. (1989) *Feminist Social Work*, Basingstoke: Macmillan.

Donnelly, A. (1986) *Feminist Social Work with a Women's Group*, Monograph 41, University of East Anglia.

Dunant, S. (ed.) (1994) *The War of the Words: The Political Correctness Debate*, London: Virago.

Edwards, J. (1998) 'Screening out men: or "has mum changed her washing powder recently?"', in J. Popay, J. Hearn and J. Edwards (eds) *Men, Gender Divisions and Welfare*, London: Routledge.

Egeland, C. (2004) 'What's feminist in feminist theory?', *European Journal of Women's Studies*, 11, 2: 177–188.

Eley, R. (1989) 'Women in management in social services', in C. Hallett (ed.) *Women and Social Services Departments*, London: Harvester Wheatsheaf.

Ellis, K., Davis, A. and Rummery, K. (1999) 'Needs assessment, street-level bureaucracy and the new community care', *Social Policy and Administration*, 33: 262–280.

Evans, D. (1985) 'Developing feminist groups in statutory practice: a case study of women's groups in "Smalltown"', unpublished MA dissertation, University of Warwick.

Evans, J. (1995) *Feminist Theory Today: An Introduction to Second-Wave Feminism*, London: Sage.

Evans, T. and Harris, J. (2004) 'Street-level bureaucracy, social work and the (exaggerated) death of discretion', *British Journal of Social Work*, 34, 6: 871–895.

Everitt, A. (1991) 'Will women managers save social work?', in P. Carter, T. Jeffs and M. Smith (eds) *Social Work Yearbook 2*, Buckingham: Open University Press.

Everitt, A. (1998) 'Research and development in social work', in R. Adams, L. Dominelli and M. Payne (eds) *Social Work: Themes, Issues and Critical Debates*, Basingstoke: Macmillan.

Falk, A. (1986) 'The process of feminist group work in statutory settings', unpublished MA dissertation, University of Warwick.

Fawcett, B. (1998) 'Disability and social work: applications from poststructuralism, postmodernism and feminism', *British Journal of Social Work*, 28, 263–277.

Fawcett, B. (2000) *Feminist Perspectives on Disability*, Harlow: Prentice Hall.

Fawcett, B., Featherstone, B., Fook, J. and Rossiter, A. (2000) *Practice and Research in Social Work: Postmodern Feminist Perspectives*, London: Routledge.

Featherstone, B. and Fawcett, B. (1995a) 'Feminism and child abuse: opening up some possibilities', *Critical Social Policy*, 42, 61–80.

Featherstone, B. and Fawcett, B. (1995b) 'Oh no! Not more isms: feminism, post-modernism, post-structuralism and social work education', *Social Work Education*, 14, 3: 25–43.

Featherstone, B. and Fawcett, B. (1995c) 'Power, difference and social work: an exploration', *Issues in Social Work Education*, 15, 1: 3–20.

Finch, J. (1984) 'It's great to have someone to talk to: the ethics and politics of interviewing women', in C. Bell and H. Roberts (eds) *Social Researching: Politics, Problems and Practice*, London: RKP.

Fook, J. (1986) 'Feminist contributions to casework practice', in H. Marchant and B. Wearing (eds) *Gender Reclaimed: Women in Social Work*, Sydney: Hale and Iremonger.

Fook, J. (1993) *Radical Casework. A Theory of Practice*, Sydney: Allen and Unwin.

Fook, J. (2002) *Social Work: Critical Theory and Practice*, London: Sage.

Forrest, D. (2000) 'Theorising empowerment thought: illuminating the relationship between ideology and politics in the contemporary era', *Sociological Research Online*, 4, 4: 1–31.

Foster, G. (2004) 'Managing front line practice. Women and men: the social care workforce', in D. Statham (ed.) *Managing Front Line Practice in Social Care*, London: Jessica Kingsley.

Fraser, N. and Nicholson, L. (1990) 'Social criticism without philosophy: an encounter between feminism and postmodernism', in L. Nicholson (ed.) *Feminism/Postmodernism*, New York: Routledge, Chapman, and Hall.

Froggett, L. and Sapey, B. (1996) 'Markets, management and social work', *Professional Social Work*, June: 9–11.

Ginn, J. and Fisher, M. (1999) 'Gender and career progression', in S. Balloch, J. McLean and M. Fisher (eds) *Social Workers under Pressure*, Bristol: Policy Press.

Graham, H. (1983) 'Do her answers fit his questions? Women and the survey method', in E. Gamarnika, D. Morgan, J. Purvis and D. Taylor (eds) *The Public and the Private*, London: Heinemann.

Graham, H. (1984) 'Surveying through stories', in C. Bell and H. Roberts (eds) *Social Researching*, London: Routledge.

Graham, H. (1992) 'Feminism and social work education', *Issues in Social Work Education*, 11, 2: 48–68.

Grey, C. (2005) *A Very Short, Fairly Interesting and Reasonably Cheap Book about Studying Organizations*, London: Sage.

GSCC (2004) *Code of Practice: Social Care Workers*, London: General Social Care Council.

Hale, J. (1984) 'Feminism and social work practice', in B. Jordan and N. Parton (eds) *The Political Dimensions of Social Work*, Oxford: Basil Blackwell.

Hall, S. (1998) 'The great moving nowhere show', *Marxism Today*, November/December, 9–14.

Hallett, C. (ed.) (1989) *Women and Social Services Departments*, Hemel Hempstead: Harvester Wheatsheaf.

Hallett, C. (1991) 'The Children Act 1989 and community care: comparisons and contrasts', *Policy and Politics*, 19, 4: 283–292.

Hallett, C. (1996) 'Social policy: continuities and change', in C. Hallett (ed.) *Women and Social Policy: An Introduction*, Hemel Hempstead: Harvester Wheatsheaf.

Hanmer, J. and Statham, D. (1999) *Women and Social Work: Towards a Woman-Centred Practice*, 2nd edn, Basingstoke: Macmillan.

Harding, S. (1990) 'Feminism, science and the anti-enlightenment critiques', in L. Nicholson (ed.) *Feminism and Postmodernism*, London: Routledge.

Harding, S. (1991) *Whose Science? Whose Knowledge? Thinking from Women's Lives*, New York: Cornell University Press.

Harlow, E. (1998) 'Gendered subjectivities: becoming managers in a social services department', unpublished Ph.D. thesis, University of Bradford.

Harlow, E. (2003) 'New managerialism, social service departments and social work practice today', *Practice*, 15, 2: 29–44.

Harlow, E. (2004) 'Why don't women want to be social workers any more? New managerialism, post-feminism and the shortage of social workers in social services departments in England and Wales', *European Journal of Social Work*, 7, 2: 167–179.

Harlow, E. and Lawlor, J. (2000) *Management, Social Work and Change*, Aldershot: Ashgate.

Harris, J. (2003) *The Social Work Business*, London: Routledge.

Healy, K. (1999) 'Power and activist social work', in B. Pease and J. Fook (eds) *Transforming Social Work Practice: Postmodern Critical Perspectives*, St Leonard's: Allen and Unwin.

Healy, K. (2000) *Social Work Practices: Contemporary Perspectives on Change*, London: Sage.

Healy, K. (2002) 'Managing human services in a market environment: what role for social workers?' *British Journal of Social Work*, 32: 527–540.

Healy, K. (2005) *Social Work Theories in Context: Creating Frameworks for Practice*, Basingstoke: Palgrave Macmillan.

Hill, M. (1997) *The Policy Process in the Modern State*, Hemel Hempstead: Harvester Wheatsheaf.

Hill Collins, P. (1991) 'Learning from the outside within: the sociological significance of black feminist thought', in M. Fonow and J. Cook (eds) *Beyond Methodology: Feminist Scholarship as Lived Research*, Indianapolis: Indiana University Press.

Hillin, A. (1985) 'When you stop hiding your sexuality', *Social Work Today*, 4: 18–19.

Hoggett, P. (1991) 'A new management in the public sector', *Policy and Politics*, 19, 4: 143–156.

Hoggett, P. (1996) 'New modes of control in the public service', *Public Administration*, 74, 3: 9–32.

hooks, b. (1990) 'Sisterhood: political solidarity between women', in S. Gunew (ed.) *Feminist Knowledge: Critique and Construct*, London: Routledge.

Horner, N. (2003) *What Is Social Work? Contexts and Perspectives*, Exeter: Learning Matters.

Howe, D. (1979) 'Agency function and social work principles', *British Journal of Social Work*, 9, 1: 29–49.

Howe, D. (1980) 'Inflated states and empty theories in social work', *British Journal of Social Work*, 10, 3: 317–340.

Howe, D. (1986) *Social Workers and their Practice in Welfare Bureaucracies*, Aldershot: Gower.

Howe, D. (1994) 'Modernity, postmodernity and social work', *British Journal of Social Work*, 24, 5: 513–532.

Howe, D. (1996) 'Surface and depth in social-work practice', in N. Parton (ed.) *Social Theory, Social Change and Social Work*, London: Routledge.

Hudson, A. (1985) 'Feminism and social work: resistance or dialogue?' *British Journal of Social Work*, 15: 635–655.

Hudson, A. (1989) 'Changing perspectives: feminism, gender and social work', in M. Langan and P. Lee (eds) *Radical Social Work Today*, London: Unwin Hyman.

Hudson, A., Ayerson, L., Oakley, C. and Patocchi, M. (1994) 'Practising feminist approaches', in T. Philpot (ed.) *Practising Social Work*, London: Routledge.

Hudson, B. (1989) 'Michael Lipsky and street-level bureaucracy: a neglected perspective', in L. Barton (ed.) *Disability and Dependency*, Brighton: Falmer Press.

Hughes, B. and Mtezuka, M. (1992) 'Social work and older women: where have older women gone?', in M. Langan and L. Day (eds) *Women, Oppression and Social Work*, London: Routledge.

Hughes, C. (2002) *Women's Contemporary Lives: Within and Beyond the Mirror*, London: Routledge.

Hugman, R. (1991a) 'Organization and professionalism: the social work agenda in the 1990s', *British Journal of Social Work*, 21: 199–216.

Hugman, R. (1991b) *Power in the Caring Professions*, Basingstoke: Macmillan.

Hugman, R. (1996) 'Professionalization in social work: the challenge of diversity', *International Social Work*, 39, 2: 199–216.

Humphrey, J.C. (2002) 'Joint reviews: retracing the trajectory, decoding the terms', *British Journal of Social Work*, 32: 463–476.

Humphrey, J.C. (2003a) 'Joint reviews: the methodology in action', *British Journal of Social Work*, 33: 177–190.

Humphrey, J.C. (2003b) 'Joint reviews: judgement day and beyond', *British Journal of Social Work*, 33: 727–738.

Humphreys, C. (1994) 'Counteracting mother-blaming among child sexual abuse service providers', *Journal of Feminist Family Therapy*, 6, 1: 49–64.

Humphries, B. (1997) 'Reading social work: competing discourses in the rules and requirements for the Diploma in Social Work', *British Journal of Social Work*, 27: 641–658.

Huntington, A. (1999) 'Child care social work and the role of state employees', *Child and Family Social Work*, 4: 241–248.

Irving, J. and Gertig, P. (1998) 'Brave new world: social workers' perceptions of care management', *Practice*, 10, 2: 5–15.

Issitt, M. and Woodward, M. (1992) 'Competence and contradiction', in P. Carter, T. Jeffs and M. Smith (eds) *Changing Social Work and Welfare*, Buckingham: Open University Press.

Itzin, C. and Newman, J. (eds) (1995) *Gender, Culture and Organizational Change: Putting Theory into Practice*, London: Routledge.

Johnson, T.J. (1972) *Professions and Power*, London: Macmillan.

Jones, C. (1989) 'The end of the road? Issues in social work education', in P. Carter, T. Jeffs and M. Smith (eds) *Social Work and Social Welfare Yearbook 1*, Buckingham: Open University Press.

Jones, C. (1993) 'Distortion and demonisation: the right and anti-racism', *Social Work Education*, 12, 3: 9–16.

Jones, C. (1995) 'Demanding social work education: an agenda for the end of the century', *Issues in Social Work Education*, 15: 3–15.

Jones, C. (1996) 'Anti-intellectualism and the peculiarities of British social work education', in N. Parton (ed.) *Social Theory, Social Change and Social Work*, London: Routledge.

Jones, C. (1999) 'Social work: regulation and managerialism', in M. Exworthy and S. Halford (eds) *Professionals and the New Managerialism in the Public Sector*, Buckingham: Open University Press.

Jones, C. (2001) 'Voices from the front line: state social workers and New Labour', *British Journal of Social Work*, 31: 547–562.

Jones, C. and Novak, T. (1994) 'Social work today', *British Journal of Social Work*, 23: 195–212.

Jones, K. (1994) *The Making of Social Policy in Britain, 1830–1990*, 2nd edn, London: Athlone Press.

Jones, M. and Jordan, B. (1996) 'Knowledge and practice in social work', in M. Preston-Shoot and S. Jackson (eds) *Educating Social Workers in a Changing Policy Context*, London: Whiting and Birch.

Jones, S. (1985) 'The analysis of depth interviewing', in R. Walker (ed.) *Applied Qualitative Research*, Aldershot: Gower.

Jordan, B. (1987) *The Common Good: Citizenship, Morality and Self-interest*, Oxford: Blackwell.

Jordan, B. (1990) *Social Work in an Unjust Society*, Hemel Hempstead: Harvester.

Jordan, B. (1991) 'Competencies and values', *Social Work Education*, 10, 1: 5–11.

Jordan, B. (2005) 'New Labour, choice and values', *Critical Social Policy*, 25, 4: 427–446.

Jordan, B. and Jordan, C. (2000) *Social Work and the Third Way: Tough Love as Social Policy*, London: Sage.

Keane, J. (1988) *Democracy and Civil Society*, London: Verso.

Kelly, A. (1992) 'The new managerialism in the social services', in P. Carter, T. Jeffs and M. Smith (eds) *Social Work and Social Welfare Yearbook 3*, Buckingham: Open University Press.

Kemp, S. and Squires, J. (1997) *Feminisms*, Oxford: Oxford University Press.

Kemshall, H. (1986) *Defining Clients' Needs in Social Work*, Norwich: University of East Anglia, Social Work Monographs.

Kravetz, K. (1976) 'Sexism in a woman's profession', *Social Work*, 21, 6: 421–426.

La Valle, I. and Lyons, K. (1996a) 'The social worker speaks I: perception of recent changes in British social work', *Practice*, 8, 2: 5–14.

La Valle, I. and Lyons, K. (1996b) 'The social worker speaks II: management of change in the personal social services', *Practice* 8, 3: 63–71.

Langan, M. (1985) 'The unitary approach: a feminist critique', in E. Brook and A. Davis (eds) *Women, the Family and Social Work*, London: Tavistock.

Langan, M. (1992a) 'Introduction: Women and Social Work in the 1990s', in M. Langan and L. Day (eds) *Women, Oppression and Social Work: Issues in Anti-discriminatory Practice*, London: Routledge.

Langan, M. (1992b) 'Who cares? Women in the mixed economy of care', in M. Langan and L. Day (eds) *Women, Oppression and Social Work: Issues in Anti-discriminatory Practice*, London: Routledge.

Langan, M. (1993) 'New directions in social work', in J. Clarke (ed.) *A Crisis in Care? Challenges to Social Work*, London: Sage.

Langan, M. (1998) 'Radical social work', in R. Adams, L. Dominelli and M. Payne (eds) *Social Work: Themes, Issues and Critical Debates*, Basingstoke: Macmillan.

Langan, M. and Day, L. (eds) (1992) *Women, Oppression and Social Work: Issues in Anti-discriminatory Practice*, London: Routledge.

Langan, M. and Lee, P. (eds) (1989) *Radical Social Work Today*, London: Unwin Hyman.

Lennon, K. and Whitford, M. (1995) *Knowing the Difference: Feminist Perspectives in Epistemology*, London: Routledge.

Leonard, P. (1996) 'Three discourses on practice: a postmodern reappraisal', *Journal of Sociology and Social Welfare*, 23, 2: 7–25.

Leonard, P. (1997a) 'Power and resistance in social service bureaucracies: Organizational issues in the debate on social citizenship,' paper presented at the *International Symposium on Social Citizenship and Social Service Work*, University of Bielefeld.

Leonard, P. (1997b) *Postmodern Welfare: Reconstructing an Emancipatory Project*, London: Sage.

Lewis, G. (1996) 'Situated voices: Black women's experiences and social work', *Feminist Review*, 53: 24–56.

Lipsky, M. (1980) *Street-level Bureaucracy*, New York: Russell Sage.

Lister, R. (2000) 'Gender and the analysis of social policy', in G. Lewis, S. Gewirtz and J. Clarke (eds) *Rethinking Social Policy*, London: Sage.

Lloyd, S. and Degenhardt, D. (1996) 'Working with male social work students', in K. Cavanagh and V. Cree (eds) *Working with Men: Feminism and Social Work*, London: Routledge.

Local Government Training Board (1985) *Good Management in Local Government: Successful Practice and Action*, Luton: Local Government Training Board.

Logan, J. and Kershaw, S. (1994) 'Heterosexism and social work education: the invisible challenge', *Social Work Education*, 13, 3: 61–80.

Lundy, M. (1993) 'Explicitness: The unspoken mandate of feminist social work', *Affilia*, 8, 2: 184–199.

Lupton, C. (1992) 'Feminism, managerialism and performance management', in M. Langan and L. Day (eds) *Women, Oppression and Social Work*, London: Routledge.

Lupton, C. (1998) 'User empowerment or family self-reliance? The family group conference model', *British Journal of Social Work*, 28, 107–128.

Lymbery, M. (1998) 'Care management and professional autonomy: the impact of community care legislation on social work with older people', *British Journal of Social Work*, 28: 863–878.

Lymbery, M. (2001) 'Social work at the crossroads', *British Journal of Social Work*, 31: 369–384.

Macey, M. and Moxon, E. (1996) 'An examination of anti-racist and anti-oppressive theory and practice in social work education', *British Journal of Social Work*, 26, 3: 297–314.

McLaughlin, K. (2005) 'From ridicule to institutionalisation: anti-oppression, the state and social work', *Critical Social Policy*, 25, 3: 283–305.

McNay, M. (1992) 'Social work and power relations: towards a framework for an integrated practice', in M. Langan and L. Day (eds) *Women's Oppression and Social Work: Issues in Anti-discriminatory Practice*, London: Routledge.

McPhail, B. (2004) 'Setting the record straight: social work is not a female-dominated profession', *Social Work*, 49, 2: 323–326.

Marchant, H. and Wearing, B. (eds) (1986) *Gender Reclaimed: Women in Social Work*, Sydney: Hale and Iremonger.

Marshall, T.H. (1965) *Social Policy*, London: Heinemann.

Marshall, T.H. (1975) *Social Policy in the Twentieth Century*, London: Hutchinson.

Marshall, T.H. (1981) *The Right to Welfare and Other Essays*, London: Heinemann.

Mashaw, J.L. (1983) *Bureaucratic Justice*, New Haven: Yale University Press.

Means, R. and Smith, R. (1998) *Community Care: Policy and Practice* (2nd edn), Basingstoke: Macmillan.

Milner, J. (1993) 'A disappearing act: the differing career paths of fathers and mothers in child protection investigations', *Critical Social Policy*, 13, 2: 48–63.

Milner, J. (1996) 'Men's resistance to social workers', in B. Fawcett, B. Featherstone,

J. Hearn and C. Toft (eds), *Violence and Gender Relations: Theories and Interventions*, London: Sage.

Milner, J. (2001) *Women and Social Work: Narrative Approaches*, Basingstoke: Palgrave.

Morris, J. (1991/92) '"Us" and "them"? Feminist research, community care and disability', *Critical Social Policy*, 33, 3: 22–39.

Morris, J. (1993) 'Women confronting disability', in J. Clarke (ed.) *A Crisis in Care? Challenges to Social Work*, London: Sage.

Morris, J. (1996) *Encounters with Strangers: Feminism and Disability*, London: The Women's Press.

Mullender, A. (1995) 'The assessment of anti-oppressive practice in the DipSW', *Issues in Social Work Education*, 15, 1: 60–66.

Mullender, A. (1997) 'Gender', in M. Davies (ed.) *The Blackwell Companion to Social Work*, Oxford: Blackwell.

NCVQ (1988) *The NCVQ Criteria and Related Guidance*, London: National Council for Vocational Qualifications.

Newman, J. (1994) 'The limits of management: gender and the politics of change', in J. Clarke, A. Cochrane and E. McLaughlin (eds) *Managing Social Policy*, London: Sage.

Newman, J. (1995) 'Gender and cultural change', in C. Itzin and J. Newman (eds) *Gender, Culture and Organizational Change: Putting Theory into Practice*, London: Routledge.

Newman, J. and Clarke, J. (1994) 'Going about our business? The managerialization of public services', in J. Clarke, A. Cochrane and E. McLaughlin (eds) *Managing Social Policy*, London: Sage.

Novak, T. (1995) 'Thinking about a new social work curriculum', *Social Work Education*, 14, 1: 4–10.

Oakley, A. (1981) 'Interviewing women: a contradiction in terms?' in H. Roberts (ed.) *Doing Feminist Research*, London: RKP.

O'Hagan, K. (1996) *Competence in Social Work Practice*, London: Jessica Kingsley.

O'Hagan, K. and Dillenburger, K. (1995) *The Abuse of Women within Child Care Work*, Buckingham: Open University Press.

Orme, J. (1998) 'Feminist social work', in R. Adams, L. Dominelli and M. Payne (eds) *Social Work: Themes, Issues and Critical Debates*, Basingstoke: Macmillan.

Orme, J. (2001) *Gender and Community Care: Social Work and Social Care Perspectives*, Basingstoke: Palgrave.

Orme, J. (2003) '"It's feminist because I say so": feminism, social work and critical practice in the UK', *Qualitative Social Work*, 2, 2: 131–153.

Otway, O. (1996) 'Social work with children and families: from child welfare to child protection', in N. Parton (ed.) *Social Theory, Social Change and Social Work*, London: Routledge.

Packman, J. and Jordan, B. (1991) 'The Children Act: looking forward, looking back', *British Journal of Social Work*, 21, 4: 315–327.

Parry, N. and Parry, J. (1979) 'Social work, professionalism and the state', in N. Parry, M. Rustin and C. Satyamurti (eds) *Social Work, Welfare and the State*, London: Edward Arnold.

Parsloe, P. and Stevenson, O. (1978) *Social Services Teams: The Practitioners' View*, London: HMSO.

Parton, N. (1994) 'Problematics of government, (post)modernity and social work', *British Journal of Social Work*, 24, 1: 9–32.

Parton, N. (1996a) 'Social theory, social change and social work: an introduction', in N. Parton (ed.) *Social Theory, Social Change and Social Work*, London: Routledge.

Parton, N. (1996b) 'Social work, risk and "the blaming system"', in N. Parton (ed.) *Social Theory, Social Change and Social Work*, London: Routledge.

Parton, N. and Marshall, W. (1998) 'Postmodernism and discourse approaches in social work', in R. Adams, L. Dominelli and M. Payne (eds) *Social Work: Themes, Issues and Critical Debates*, Basingstoke: Macmillan.

Payne, M. (1994) 'Partnership between organisations in social work education', *Issues in Social Work Education* 14, 1: 53–70.

Payne, M. (1995) *Social Work and Community Care*, Basingstoke: Macmillan.

Pease, B. (2002) 'Rethinking empowerment: a postmodern reappraisal for emancipatory practice', *British Journal of Social Work*, 32, 2: 135–147.

Pease, B. and Fook, J. (1999) *Transforming Social Work Practice*, London: Routledge.

Pell, L. and Scott, D. (1995) 'The cloak of competence: assessment dilemmas in social work education', *Social Work Education*, 14, 4: 38–57.

Phillips, M. (1993) 'Oppressive urge to end oppression', *Observer*, 1 August.

Phillipson, J. (1991) *Practising Equality: Women, Men and Social Work*, London: Central Council for Education and Training in Social Work.

Philp, M. (1979) 'Notes on the form of knowledge in social work', *Sociological Review*, 27, 1: 83–111.

Pithouse, A. (1987) *Social Work: The Social Organisation of an Invisible Trade*, Aldershot: Gower.

Pithouse, A. (1991) 'Guardians of autonomy: work orientations in a social work office', in P. Carter, T. Jeffs and S. Smith (eds) *Social Work and Social Welfare Yearbook 2*, Buckingham: Open University Press.

Pollitt, C. (1990) *Managerialism and the Public Services: The Anglo-American Experience*, Oxford: Blackwell.

Postle, K. (2001) 'The social work side is disappearing. I guess it started with us being called care managers', *Practice*, 13, 1: 13–26.

Postle, K. (2002) 'Working "between the idea and the reality": ambiguities and tensions in care managers' work', British Journal of Social Work, 32: 335–351.

Preston-Shoot, M. (1995) 'Assessing anti-oppressive practice', *Social Work Education*, 14, 2: 11–29.

Preston-Shoot, M. (1996) 'A question of emphasis? On legalism and social work education', in M. Preston-Shoot and S. Jackson (eds) *Educating Social Workers in a Changing Policy Context*, London: Whiting and Birch.

QAA (2000) *Social Policy and Administration and Social Work*, benchmark statement, Gloucester: Quality Assurance Agency.

Ramazanoglu, C. (1986) 'Ethnocentrism and socialist-feminist theory: a response to Barrett and McIntosh', *Feminist Review*, 22: 83–6.

Reynolds, J. (1994) 'Introducing gender issues into social work education: is this just women's work?' *Issues in Social Work Education*, 14, 2: 3–20.

Reynolds, J. (1997) 'Feminist theory and strategy in social work', in J. Walmsley, J. Reynolds, P. Shakespeare and R. Woolfe (eds) *Health, Welfare and Practice*, London: Sage.

Roche, M. (1987) 'Citizenship, social theory and social change', *Theory and Society*, 16: 363–399.

Roche, M. (1992) *Rethinking Citizenship: Welfare, Ideology and Change in Modern Society*, Cambridge: Polity Press.

Rojek, C., Peacock, G. and Collins, S. (1988) *Social Work and Received Ideas*, London: Macmillan.

Sakamato, I. and Pitner, R.O. (2005) 'Use of critical consciousness in anti-oppressive social work practice: disentangling power dynamics at personal and structural levels', *British Journal of Social Work*, 35: 435–452.

Sands, R. and Nuccio, K. (1992) 'Postmodern feminist theory and social work', *Social Work*, 37, 6: 489–494.

Satyamurti, C. (1981) *Occupational Survival*, Oxford: Blackwell.

Seebohm Report (1968) *Report of the Committee on Local Authority and Allied Personal Social Services*, cmnd 3708, London: HMSO.

Seed, P. (1973) *The Expansion of Social Work in Great Britain*, London: Routledge & Kegan Paul.

Shah, N. (1989) 'It's up to you sisters: black women and radical social work', in M. Langan and P. Lee (eds) *Radical Social Work Today*, London: Unwin Hyman.

Sheppard, M. (1995) *Care Management and the New Social Work: A Critical Analysis*, London: Whiting and Birch.

Showstack-Sassoon, A. (1987) 'Introduction: the personal and the intellectual, fragments and order, international trends and national specificities', in A. Showstack-Sassoon (ed.) *Women and the State*, London: Routledge.

Sibeon, R. (1991) *Towards a New Sociology of Social Work*, Aldershot: Avebury.

Skeggs, B. (2001) *Formations of Class and Gender*, London: Sage.

Smith, G. (1980) *Social Need: Policy, Practice and Research*, London: Routledge & Kegan Paul.

SSI (Social Services Inspectorate) (2002) *Modern Social Services: A Commitment to Reform. 11th Annual Report of the Chief Inspector of Social Services*, London: Department of Health.

Stanley, L. (ed.) (1990) *Feminist Praxis*, London: Routledge.

Stanley, L. (1997) *Knowing Feminisms: On Academic Borders, Territories and Tribes*, London: Sage.

Stanley, L. and Wise, S. (1990) 'Method, methodology and epistemology in feminist research processes', in L. Stanley (ed.) *Feminist Praxis*, London: Routledge.

Stanley, L. and Wise, S. (1993) *Breaking Out Again: Feminist Ontology and Epistemology*, London: Routledge.

Statham, D. (2004) *Managing Frontline Practice in Social Care*, London: Jessica Kingsley.

Statham, D. (1979) *Radicals in Social Work*, London: Routledge & Kegan Paul.

Statham, D. and Carroll, G. (1994) 'Diploma document does not ignore race', *Community Care*, 27 October, letter to editor.

Taylor, C. and White, S. (2000) *Practising Reflexivity in Health and Welfare: Making Knowledge*, Buckingham: Open University Press.

Thomas, R. and Davies, A. (2005) 'What have the feminists done for us? Feminist theory and organizational resistance', *Organization*, 12, 5: 711–740.

Thompson, N. (1993) *Anti-discriminatory Practice*, Basingstoke: Macmillan.

Timms, N. (1991) 'A new Diploma for Social Work or Dunkirk as total victory', in P. Carter, T. Jeffs and M. Smith (eds) *Social Work and Social Welfare Yearbook 3*, Buckingham: Open University Press.

TOPSS (2004) *The National Occupational Standards for Social Work*, Leeds: Training Organisation for the Personal Social Services.

TOPSS (2005) Online. Available HTTP: <http://www.topssengland.net/view.asp?id=36>. Accessed 18 October.

Trotter, J. and Gilchrist, J. (1996) 'Assessing DipSW students: anti-discriminatory practice in relation to lesbian and gay issues', *Social Work Education*, 15, 1: 75–82.

University of Warwick (1978) *Preparing for Social Work Practice: A Contribution to the Unfinished Debate on Social Work and Social Work Education,* Coventry: University of Warwick, Department of Applied Social Studies.

Walton, R. (2005) 'Social work as a social institution', *British Journal of Social Work*, 35: 587–607.

Ward, D. and Mullender, A. (1991) 'Empowerment and oppression: an indissoluble pairing for contemporary social work', *Critical Social Policy*, 32: 21–30.

Warren, L. (1985) *Older Women and Feminist Social Work Practice*, Critical Social Work Monographs, Coventry: University of Warwick.

Watson, S. (1999) 'Engendering social policy: an introduction', in S.Watson and L. Doyal (eds) *Engendering Social Policy*, Buckingham: Open University Press.

Watt, S. and Cooke, J. (1989) 'Another expectation unfulfilled: black women and social services departments', in C. Hallett (ed.) *Women and Social Services Departments*, Hemel Hempstead: Harvester Wheatsheaf.

Webb, D. (1991) 'Puritans and paradigms: a speculation on the form of new moralities in social work', *Social Work and Social Sciences Review*, 2, 2: 146–159.

Webb, D. (1996) 'Regulations for radicals: The state, CCETSW and the academy', in N. Parton (ed.) *Social Theory, Social Change and Social Work*, London: Routledge.

Webb, A. and Wistow, G. (1987) *Social Work, Social Care and Social Planning: The Personal Social Services since Seebohm*, Harlow: Longman.

White, V. and Harris, J. (2001) *Developing Good Practice in Community Care: Partnership and Participation*, London: Jessica Kingsley.

White, V. and Harris, J. (2004) *Developing Good Practice in Children's Services*, London: Jessica Kingsley.

Wilding, P. (1982) *Professional Power and Social Welfare*, London: Routledge & Kegan Paul.

Williams, C. (1999) 'Connecting anti-racist and anti-oppressive theory and practice: retrenchment or reappraisal? *British Journal of Social Work*, 29: 211–230.

Williams, F. (1992) 'Women with learning difficulties are women too', in M. Langan and L. Day (eds) *Women, Oppression and Social Work: Issues in Anti-discriminatory Practice*, London: Routledge.

Williams, F. (1996) 'Postmodernism, feminism and difference', in N. Parton (ed.) *Social Theory, Social Change and Social Work*, London: Routledge.

Wilson, E. (1975) 'Feminism and social work', in R. Bailey and M. Brake (eds) *Radical Social Work*, London: Edward Arnold.

Wise, S. (1985) 'Becoming a feminist social worker', in L. Stanley (ed.) *Feminist Praxis*, London: Routledge.

Wise, S. (1995) 'Feminist ethics in practice', in R. Hugman and D. Smith (eds) *Ethical Issues in Social Work*, London: Routledge.

Witz, A. (1992) *Patriarchy and Professions*, London: Routledge.

Wootton, B. (1959) *Social Science and Social Pathology*, London: Allen and Unwin.

Wright, R. (1977) *Expectations of the Teaching of Social Work in Courses Leading to the Certificate of Qualification in Social Work: Consultative Document Number Three,* London: Central Council for Education and Training in Social Work.

Youll, P. (1996) 'Managerialism and social work education', in M. Preston-Shoot and S. Jackson (eds) *Educating Social Workers in a Changing Policy Context*, London: Whiting and Birch.

Index